The Last Call

"Anyone who looks upon the face of My holy statue will receive from My Son and I an imprint on his heart and soul and will have peace of mind".

"And for those who cannot come and see the holy image in person, they can obtain beautiful pictures of the Madonna of Fatima for their homes; they will be greatly protected from fire, storms and the malice of man".

"This is My promise, through the Immaculate Heart of Your Mother".

Mary
May 1981

JEAN-YVES SIMARD

THE LAST CALL

Translated by
Brother Joseph Matthew

*"My tears speak louder than
My words..."*
(Message of April 5, 1984)

*"... whereof all we are
witnesses."*
(Acts 2, 32)

LES ÉDITIONS FATIMA-QUÉBEC

Exclusive Publishing House of
The Pillars and Servants
of the Immaculate Heart of Mary

P.O. Box 7515
Charlesbourg, Que.   G1G 5W5
Canada

This volume is a translation of
LE DERNIER APPEL by Jean-Yves Simard,
published by Les Éditions Fatima-Québec,
Charlesbourg, Que.

Legal Deposit: 3rd quarter 1985
National Library of Canada
National Library of Quebec

ISBN 2-920813-01-3

*In Filial Homage
to the Immaculate Heart of Mary
Refuge
of All Souls*

Declaration

All the facts and messages related herein have been reported as faithfully as possible from the narration of those who have seen and heard, mainly the privileged messenger. The content of this book is of private testimonial value resting on the sincerity and veracity of the persons concerned, and in no way presumes on the judgement of the Church.

If there is any error in the account of the facts or in their interpretations, this would be an overlook by the author and his collaborators, and they beforehand submit to any rectification which could be asked of them.

Regarding the official authentication of the signs, the miracles, or other facts reputedly miraculous, and also of the commentaries and interpretations on them, we rely on the authorized judgement of the Church, to which we are and wish to remain devotedly submissive.

The Author and His Collaborators

* * *

Favors Obtained

It is for the glory of God and the triumph of the Immaculate Heart of Mary that this work has been written. It is also for the same aims that we make known the manifestations of the Divine goodness and mercy of which this book is strewn. If certain things must remain hidden, it is in order to manifest to God our gratitude as would the numerous sick that Jesus cured spiritually and physically during His life on earth.

So anyone who will have received, or will receive spiritual or temporal favors by the intercession of the Weeping Madonna, through Her photos, or by the intermediary of Her messenger, is asked to make it known to us, by writing to the editor of this work. To precise all the circumstances surrounding the favor obtained, this comprising medical declarations in the case of important cures.

Please write to:

Secretariat F.O.
Les Éditions Fatima-Québec
P.O. Box 7515
Charlesbourg, Qué., G1G 5W5
Canada

Thank you, in the name of the Immaculate Heart of Mary!

STATEMENT OF ANONYMITY

The main advocate in this book is without question the Blessed Virgin Mary, Mother of God and Mother of the Church. These pages are the echo of the pathetic cry of Her Immaculate Heart pouring out, in Her tears and messages, the final calls to the whole world. What does She desire else the salvation of souls and the return to God of the innumerous throngs who live in a neopaganism without precedent in history?

The second proponent emerging through the narration is Her witness, Her confidant, the keeper of the "weeping statue", who entreats us to keep him out of the light. If it is impossible for us to pass under silence his experience, and if certain salient traits of his life must of necessity be revealed, we readily accede to his wish that his name be concealed in anonymity.

As his great desire is to live religiously, under an identity recalling two great protectors to whom he confides his life and testimony, we shall designate him, according to his request, as Brother JOSEPH FRANCIS.

DECREE

The Decree from the Congregation for the Propagation of the Faith n. 58/16, of the 29th of December, 1966, had been already approved by His Holiness Paul VI on the 14th of October of the same year, and was published upon his personal decision. Three months later, the Decree was ratified. Therefore, it is not forbidden to publish without "imprimatur" any document related with apparitions, visions and miracles.

PREFACE

At the beginning of the world, God Himself communicated His Will to the first man whom He had just created and established as king of creation and head of humanity. Having thus directly spoken to our first parents, and afterwards to Abraham, He later transmitted His ten commandments to Moses, then chosen as the mouthpiece of the Creator. Following this, the chosen people not having always been faithful, Yahweh entrusted to certain chosen men, the prophets, the task of restoring the paths and announcing the outlines of the redemption plan.

Isais, for one, gave the immediate sign of the coming of the awaited Messiah: *"Behold a virgin shall conceive, and bear a son, and his name shall be called Emmanuel."* (Is. 7, 14)

This Son, the Word made flesh to redeem all men, will say a very significant word before giving out His Spirit to the Father. To Mary: *"... behold thy son."* To John: *"Behold thy mother."* (Jn. 19, 26-27)

Mary's role, as Mother of God and Mother of the redeemed, is therefore inscribed in the Revelation. It *had been announced* at the beginning, after the fall. It *became reality* at the Annunciation, at the moment of Mary's consent. And then *becomes explicit* at the moment of her very maternal intervention at Cana, through her word so full of meaning: *"Whatsoever he shall say to you, do ye."* (Jn. 2, 5)

Mary does not desire anything else but to bring us back to Her Son and the observance of His Word. Is She not the *Queen of prophets*?

This prophetic role of Mary, as Mother of God and Mother of the redeemed by Divine will, and as Mother of Mercy in the plan of the Redemption, it is not given to men to change or to render void. Rather they must accept it with all their being, intelligence and free will, according to the divine plan.

The Blessed Virgin has thus the right and the power to urge us to return to Her Son by appealing to our mind and our heart. Is this privilege not entailed in Her role as co-redemptrix which She has freely accepted to assume at the time of the Incarnation?

The Church in her wisdom does not make it an obligation for us to believe in private revelations, even when she recognizes them as being of supernatural origin, but she does not forbid us to believe and take notice when these relate to the content of the Revelation in a natural or organic fashion, or actualize it. The Church, in this matter, wishes first of all to make sure that the facts, the words, do not come into conflict with the dogmas, the moral standards, the Gospel and its interpretation as proclaimed and defended by the Church, under the authority of the visible head.

So therefore, if in these troubled times we are going through it happens that the Blessed Virgin Mary deigns to manifest Her presence among us, as She has often done in other countries in the past, and now from our country sends out to the entire world a *last call*, let us receive this sign of solicitude from Heaven with good will and gratitude, and may our life be transformed!

March 25, 1985   Father Jean-Paul Bélanger
On the Feast of the Annunciation

I

Chapter 1

THE CAUSE OF MY TEARS

Will the present generation at last become aware of this unproclaimed fact in history, this fact of capital importance: the active presence on earth of the Mother of God? And the grandiose Mission heavy with consequences that she is accomplishing?

For over one hundred and fifty years she has been there, near us, drawing the attention of our souls, talking asking, exhorting, pleading in every way. To what end? In order to obtain from man his conversion, his return to God and His laws.

To accomplish this task she has multiplied the most astonishing miraculous signs, invaluable favors, signs of the greatest mercy. But all this has remained practically with no effect. She finds herself constrained today to take a yet more decisive measure: She comes in tears. And she asks herself, and asks us: "My words having not born results, will my tears succeed in touching the heart of man?"

Without detaining on the multiple apparitions which have preceded the manifestations of her tears, let us retrace broadly the itinerary which Mary has followed during this century and a half among us.

First of All in Paris...

The very humble Mary often chooses what is the most little to receive and transmit her messages. In 1830, in Paris, it is to a humble sister that she showed herself and asked to have a medal engraved. The request was transmitted to her director who accepted to have it done. The miraculous medal multiplied itself and soon was around the world. The spiritual and temporal miracles were countless. The little nun, according to her wish and that of the Lord, remained out of sight. She continued, humble among the humble, to busy herself with the modest work of the community, the garden and at the infirmary.

La Salette...

At La Salette, on September 19, 1846, it is two shepherds,Melanie Calvat and Maximin Giraud who had the favor and the heavy mission to transmit to the people of God the live reproof of the Mother of the Church:

"If my people do not want to submit, I am forced to let go of my Son's arm. It is so strong and heavy that I cannot hold it any longer. For all the time I have suffered for you! I wish that my Son does not abandon you, so I am entrusted to beseech Him without cease in your behalf, and you do not pay attention..."

What sorrow in these words: "You do not pay any attention..."!

Mistrustful at first, the two children come closer, and let their pity arise in front of the this *Lady in tears* who looks like a "servant who would be a Queen".

They also see in Her a "mother whose children would have beaten and who would have fled in the mountain to cry all her want". Already at La Salette, therefore, does the Virgin weep! She will have used all the different forms of the language to recall to a faithless and lawless humanity thinking of rejoicing only, the importance of repentance, of penance and the return to God.

Lourdes...

At Lourdes, Mary identifies herself: "I am the Immaculate Conception."

Then she asks Bernadette: "Go and drink at the fountain, and wash yourself."

A symbolical request and gesture: was it not to a sinful humanity that the Mother of the Savior was asking to "wash itself in the Blood of Her Son" and to "drink to the live waters" promised in the Gospel to those who are thirsty!

Pontmain...

At Pontmain, in 1871, She recommends: "But pray my children, God will grant your prayer shortly."

Fatima...

It is at Fatima mainly that the Blessed Virgin will define more clearly the meaning of her mission and the Will of Heaven.

On June 13, after the terrible vision of hell, She again says: "... it is to save souls from damnation that the Lord wants to establish in the world the devotion to the Immaculate Heart of Mary."

It is therefore the mission of the Co-Redemptrix that Mary is accomplishing now. She is called upon to save these myriads of souls on the road to perdition, for whom the Son has shed his Blood. In sheer waste if the Mission of the Mother is not accomplished, and in sheer waste also if the world scorns her and turns away from her.

At last, on October 13 during the last of the six apparitions, Our Lady comes once more insisting on the main objective of her mission on the Portuguese soil:

"I am the Lady of the Rosary. I have come to exhort the faithful to change their lives, not to afflict by sin Our Lord already offended too much, to recite the Holy Rosary, to amend themselves and to do penance for their sins. I wish that a chapel be erected in this place in my honor."

The Tears...

The sad spectacle the present generation offers us compells to admit that up till now the mission of the Virgin has not born any fruits. She must therefore, on one hand, extend to the whole world her manifestations, and, on the other, adopt the ultimate form of language: tears!

Mary Co-Redemptrix sees herself constrained to reveal visually to the entire world the immense grief of the Sorrowful and Immaculate Heart in front of the refusals of her children to accept her messages.

Thus, a *LAST CALL.*

In a recent message addressed to priests and laymen, her favorite members of the Marian Movement, she said:

"... in these times I am appearing in Europe, in Asia, in Africa, in America, and in distant Oceania. The whole world is wrapped in my maternal mantle." (1)

The same day she added in the same message:

Look at my merciful eyes which shed tears of sorrow and compassion. In so many parts of the world I give this sign, causing copious tears to stream from my eyes, even tears of blood." (2)

A few years before, she had said:

"My tears are shed in many places to bring the entire world back to the Sorrowful Heart of your Mother."

"The tears of a mother succeed in moving the most hardened hearts. But now my tears, even tears of blood, leave many of my children completely indifferent." (3)

Will the tears of the Blessed Virgin leave us indifferent? What shall we do? What will you do, you who will read what follows?

Shall we leave without an answer this "LAST CALL" of the Mother of Mercy, of the Mother of Sorrow?

Chapter 2

THE WITNESS

It is in a city of modest size in Eastern Canada that Our Lady, one day, cast her eyes in search of a confidant for her messages and a witness to her tears.

Joseph Francis, the name we shall give him in order to respect his desire for anonymity, was called to have compassion for the tears of the Virgin, and to share her anxiety at the sight of the million of souls who are losing themselves and are threatened with hell.

He has accepted generously the thorny role of being a *prophet*, as must be called all those designated to transmit to the world the requests or warnings of Heaven.

Birth

Joseph Francis was born on Sunday, May 21, 1944. He was the second of a pair of twins, the first having been born around 5 p.m. His birth followed that of his brother by a quarter of an hour.

But his arrival was not expected: the doctor having noticed but one heart beat, only one child was anticipated. The mother was happy with the unexpected birth; the father, much less. He conceived for the undesired child a profound aversion he never sought to lessen or hide. Joseph Francis, rejected by his father, keeps for him a filial affection and an undaunted respect. The family will come to number 11 children: 7 boys and 4 girls.

The mother chooses herself the names of the twins. They are baptized one week after birth. Later, a fire will destroy the records, and at confirmation time, with no more proof of his baptism, Joseph Francis is baptized a second time under condition.

Born of a Scotch father who is a Baptist, and a Catholic mother, Joseph Francis bears in him a seed of ecumenism which will render him open towards all souls whatever their religion. He feels at ease with people of all religious denominations.

A Mother Descended from Heaven...

Having herited a delicate constitution, he was marked by suffering early. At the age of four, his parents had to have him hospitalized.

During his stay in the hospital, he was "adopted" by a mysterious lady who came to visit him regularly.

As she came in the middle of the night, and remained visible to everyone the first time, this singular presence at midnight aroused a certain emotion among the personnel. Afterward she hid her presence from their sight and showed herself to her protégé only.

She encouraged him, promising that everything would be all right. She sang beautiful hymns to him, tucked him in bed as would a mother on earth for her child. She chased all loneliness which had choked him at the beginning of his stay at the hospital.

After his return home, he continued to benefit from the visits of this "beautiful lady, so kind and gentle" who seemed as if he had always known, so much so that she became part of his life and his heart. She would urge him to go and ask his mother if he could go to church with her. There, she would teach him to genuflect, and how to pray; she would talk about her "Son" who was present, there, behind the tabernacle door. And with what affection would she speak of Him!

She complained about how her "Son" was alone, how he felt lonely, and that nearly nobody paid attention to him... During these catechism lessons, he therefore learned from her the mystery of the Eucharist: that the bread became the Body of Christ; that the wine became his blood. And she told him that he would have to nourrish himself with the Body of Christ in order to bear the trials in life. In his life, because his life *would be that of the cross...*

She also taught him many other things. For example, regarding the holy angels. And in front of the statue representing St. Joseph, she told him that he was not as old as he was portrayed ordinarily.

This "Mother" initiated him to the practice of prayer, and very early he acquired the habit by looking at the beautiful things in nature, things which he loved so much! these things which spoke about the Creator, which elevated, towards Heaven, his little heart wide open to the spiritual planes.

His mother, intrigued at the sight of this person interested in her son, asked herself who she was.

At the questions she asked, the child could only answer that he did not know her name, but that she was very good and gentle, that she had beautiful eyes, that she paid attention to him and to what he said and did, and to what happened to him, that she laughed at some of his answers, that she initiated

3

May 1980
"How many thorns afflict my Heart"
(Message to Don Gobbi, 28/12/1973)

4   May 1981

Let me mingle tears with thee…

(Stabat Mater)

5   October 1982

Through her tears, she looked up to heaven

(Dan. 13, 35)

Hear my prayer, O Lord, to my cry give ear;
to my weeping be not deaf!

(Ps. 39, 13)

7   August 21, 1984

At the time of the weeping for Fr. Jean-Paul Bélanger
An aura surrounds the statue.
Woman, why are you weeping?

(Jn. 20, 13)

8   August 24, 1984
This photo reveals the presence of a supernatural light,
which Mary will use from now on, to take the photos.
(See Part II, Chapter. 5, "Mysterious Photos")

9   August 24, 1984

Photo taken, on August 24, 1984, right after the preceding photo. The ball of light in front of the statue, becomes a swirl of light. From that date, the photo can be taken in complete darkness without any natural or artificial lighting.

10   October 1984

For this photo the light was dimmed, to let see the traces
left by the sorrows and the contusions caused the insults
(Explanation given April 21, 1985)

him to prayer. This, translated to us, means: she behaved like a "mother who would have descended from heaven...", specially to give a christian education to this child marked by a particular grace.

So Poor and So Rich!

Already, so young and very advanced on the spiritual paths, Joseph Francis has discovered on the lips of this all maternal Lady the strong and severe words of Christian austerity. He would have, as she told him, to live a "normal" life, but a life imprinted by the presence of God. A life ordinary and out of the ordinary at the same time. And that he would have to walk in the steps of Jesus.

Later he will discover what these words hid: misunderstanding, contradictions, persecution. Nailed to the cross, he also would become, in dependence on Christ, a sign of contradiction.

The beautiful Lady instructed him in all kinds of ways. One day, She told him the life of the Holy Family. He learned how Jesus, Mary and Joseph rich in God were poor in material wealth. And she predicted to him that he would have to live this material poverty alongside the greatest spiritual wealth.

Throughout these teachings, she sang beautiful songs, songs he had never heard, songs of praise and love of God. Songs exalting the Lamb of God, the Innocent Lamb, immolated for the sins of the world.

So early and vividly seized by the Lord, this child would he be like the others? It would have been a wonder.

Detached from the Earth

Different he has been. And ordinary humanity, heavy with its sloths and attachments, has difficulty to accept that certain subjects elevate themselves above the common mediocrity. Their innocence, their detachment from all things, is a constant accusation against those who are riveted to the earth.

Little Joseph Francis was rejected and held in contempt, not because of the wickedness of those around him, but because of this law which rules that all those who are marked by the prophetic seal must undergo the same destiny as that of Christ: sent by the Father to save all men, He was a capital sign of contradiction and incurred the most ignominious persecution that any man ever had to endure.

The one who lets himself be attracted towards the essential soon discovers the vanity of material things. Young Joseph Francis did not like to participate in the games of his age. One day, he gave his marbles to his twin brother. He would go pray and sing the praises of the Lord while his comrades devoted themselves to their childish activities. He naturally displayed, without wanting to show or hide it, his contempt for the amusements of childhood, and later, of youth. And this trait, on top of others of the same kind, made him more "a child not like the others".

The lack of interest for temporal things transposed itself to the school level. Studies had no attraction for him. He had to repeat his classes. The frequent moving and changing of school was not to straighten things back. All this increased the contempt he was subject to.

Scapegoat

He often was submitted to punishments without reason or as the scapegoat, through the malice of the real culprits clever in turning away on those who are the laughing-stock the consequences of their mischiefs.

His gentleness, his candor made him an easy prey to all the unkindnesses coming from his surroundings and which assailed him. He frequently underwent the punishments deserved by others. One school teacher reputed for her harshness towards kids, took a dislike to him and he met with mockery and mistreatments for no other motive than the sick need she felt to make children with no defence suffer. Incapable of grudge, Joseph Francis recounts this as items he would have preferred forgotten had he not been pressed to reveal his background.

If he often benefited from the visit of the "beautiful Lady", other celestial visitors appeared to him also: saints, angels and Jesus Himself.

It also happened that he "sensed God's presence". He was then quickly drawn to isolate himself in the woods, far from any human presence in order to sing the praises of God in all quietness.

Spiritual Education

At Mary's school, spiritual education is both strong and gentle.

Strong because the Virgin communicates her own virtues to the soul who entrusts itself to her, in such a way that this soul benefits from a participation in the very life of our Mother. Her humility, her gentleness, her strength against temptations, her prudence to avoid the snares of the Wicked One, her moderation in the use of the goods of this world, her justice in the accomplishment of daily duties, and above all the practice of the theological virtues, faith, hope, charity: all what the soul must practice is singularly found reinforced by the very action of the Mother who watches over this soul and takes part in its spiritual progress.

Gentle too is the spiritual training under Mary's guidance, in this sense that the Virgin soothes the wounds and reduces the virulence of the Devil's sting. She is always present during difficult moments, she prevents the falls by holding the soul as the mother supports the tottering first steps of a little child; the trials, under Mary's guidance, are not any less hard, but they are better endured because the maternal assistance is never lacking at each stage of life.

Joseph Francis benefited from this maternal solicitude. Opposed by a father who did not accept that his son frequented the Catholic Church, the latter had to accomplish his religious duties secretly. Discovered, a spanking awaited him. At other times, it was contempt or mockery. The special graces he benefited from already and which multiplied steadily with time, cost him dearly!

Way of the Cross

He had erected a wooden cross in the woods close to this parents' home. There was the refuge and the silent witness of his prayers and his songs of praise to the Glory of the All High. One day, he takes the pastor of the parish to see this cross. Alas! It is reduced to cinders. The priest, visibly inspired, gave him the following lesson: "The cross will always be in front of you; you will often have to carry it..."

Up to this day, Joseph Francis' whole life has been an unending way of the cross. With the consoling presence of the Mother of Sorrows, holding him by the hand. Today, and for a little over seven years, it is in tears that she reveals to him the bitter depth of her great sorrow: how lightly present humanity takes the salvation offered by her Son, and the contemptuous refusal of the infinite Mercy offered by the Father - the last plank of safety, Mary Co-Redemptrix, Mediatrix and Advocate.

The mystery of Joseph Francis' life - why not say it outright - is the choice Our Lady has made of this little one among the little to be her confidant, the witness able to attest of the reality of her tears, the faithful soul accepting to sympathize, the *loving and submissive son*, attentive to her call, and the *docile prophet,* invited to project her lament to the four corners of this country, of this world, in search of souls of good will.

Apostle

Convinced of his faith, Joseph Francis became convincing. He sought to bring his friends to the Catholic Church. He taught them prayer and penance. To forestall temptations of the flesh, he practiced the discipline, calling upon his friend to "hold and wield the whip". "Thirty-three", he would order the one hesitating, "thirty-three lashes in honor of the thirty-three years of Our Lord's life on earth."

In his childish naïveté he taught cathechism to his dog he found bad towards strangers. Little by little, the animal became more docile, more sociable, to the great displeasure of his father who did not accept the change of character in his ferocious guardian! Here one thinks of the famous *fioretti* of St. Francis of Assisi who knew so well how to mobilize the birds and animals of the forest to sing the glory of God, and who, one day, literally converted a cruel wolf that terrorized the small town of Gubbio.

At the beginning of his youth, he feels strongly drawn by *a devotion to Our Lady*. All that concerns her interests him. One day, a sermon given by a Redemptorist Father made on him a deep impression. He suffered greatly to learn that Protestantism did not accept the Catholic devotion towards the Blessed Virgin, and paid little attention to the privileges of the Mother of God, namely her Immaculate Conception.

Impossible Confidence

His apostolic desire sometimes pushed him to communicate to his brother and his friends the beautiful "things" he was learning in his experiences with the Next World. On some occasions he opened up with those close to him and in whom he trusted. He was surprised to find out that the others did not seem to have the benefit of these experiences that he on his part judged as ordinary, as they were so much part of his life. His revelations were not well taken. They believed, he says, that having climbed a tree, "he had fallen on his noddle". This embedded a new thorn. But he already knew, although an adolescent, that he would have to walk the abrupt road of calvary. If he already suspected it to be rough, he did not yet know how the brambles would whip his face and the roughness of the road damage all his limbs.

Ignoring the mockeries of which he was made the target each time he thought it opportune to broach the subject, he one day recorded on cassette some sequences of his life for the least astonishing, and passed on this narrative to the pastor mentioned above.

After having listened to this recording, the priest consoled him while at the same time announcing him something else he then judged to be less comforting: "Our Lady", said the priest, "is not through with you!"

Premonitory Signs

Indeed Our Lady was not through with Joseph Francis. She was preparing him in a virile manner to his role of witness. And God does not mould a future witness of the Beyond in no other way than through suffering, the ascetic part, and celestial communications, the mystic part. Asceticism and mysticism are the two feet of the prophet called upon to bring to the world the warnings and messages he holds from God.

Joseph Francis will want just the same to lead the normal life of an engaged lay person. Penance and mortification, accepted in a Christian way and often sought, are his daily lot. Chased from the family home, he will live for a few years with his twin brother. Later, at the death of this one, who is carried away by the lingering sequels of an auto accident, he will move to a small abode, poor and not well-heated, his revenues then reduced to their simplest expression.

Of cheerful disposition, and loving nature, singing and music, is he conscious of the heroic life he is leading? No doubt: his senses are not passive! He has to console him all these celestial beings who come to visit him one after the other and who have become his intimates.

His Vocation

Sensing that Heaven is calling him for something, he decides to take the Virgin's side and to work towards the triumph of Her Immaculate Heart. Otherwise, why would she have kept him company so often and for so long since his infancy? And why this training of a mystical order, if there is not some superior motive?

He therefore tries, through his own personal endeavors, to seek his vocation, not in a precipitated or nervous fashion, but with calm and restraint in reflection.

One day, he will understand that his vocation inclines him towards Our Lady of Fatima. In the meantime, other doors seem to open before him.

At the Monastery

What a more natural reaction, for the one whom God is calling, to serve Him in a Church institution, than to turn his sight towards convents or monasteries? Joseph Francis, at the time of his adolescence, had, on many occasions, the idea to direct his steps towards the religious life. At 16, he makes an application to enter a monastery of a Franciscan order, but a series of providential events convince him that God did not call him there.

Another day, following his request, a Trappist Abbey receives him in his monastery. This time sickness appeared and became the decisive sign that Providence was giving him to indicate clearly that his vocation was not within these walls.

These experiences, apparently negatives, carried with them certain signs of orientation. They engaged him towards lay institutions.

Marian Institutions

He came in relation with the Blue Army of Our Lady of Fatima. His zeal for the reign of the Blessed Virgin incited him to try to introduce the International Pilgrim Virgin in his diocese. In 1964, he undertook to have a petition signed inviting the diocesan authorities to make a request to that effect to the Secretariat of the Blue Army. But to no avail. Subsequent numerous steps remained fruitless. We were then in the aftermath of the council, when everywhere in the Church, in an unfortunate general fashion, the Virgin was doused as if the marian devotion had become a thing of the past.

All his efforts, spread over a period of eight years, remained in vain.

One day, he came in communications with an American author who was preparing a book on the Pilgrim Virgin. In 1967, at the time of his efforts in favor of the Pilgrim Virgin, he had conceived the plan to buy at his own expense a statue of Our Lady of Fatima in order to celebrate the 50th anniversary of the apparitions on Portuguese soil.

In 1972, an unheard-of event is brought to this knowledge, the International Pilgrim, on a visit to New Orleans, had shed some tears. At the time, the Blessed Virgin was starting to lift the veil on the role he would soon have to play.

He wanted to involve himself more actively in the Blue Army of Our Lady of Fatima. A sign turned him aside to lead him to a point beyond the efforts already done in favor of the Pilgrim Virgin. Some friends working in the Legion of Mary pressed him to join them. He did not answer the invitation definitely again feeling that the Virgin did not call him in that kind of apostolate.

He was put in relation with another Marian association. Inclined through providential signs, he joined it for a while. Following some difficulties of which he was a victim and in no way responsible, he had to cut off and pull away.

In Heaven's Grasp

From that precocious moment onwards when, at the age of four, he had been adopted by Our Lady, and she had brought him under her protective mantle, Joseph Francis was not of the earth entirely. A corner of Heaven had been revealed to him, taking away all his earthly desires, and leaving him with a taste for spiritual things only.

It is only at the age of 33 that his long period of preparation will open to the essential event of his life. In the meantime, he will have to plod on under the vigilant eye and tender protection of the Mother of the Church.

Our Lady does not come empty handed. Co-Redemptrix, She brings suffering with Her, but also the promises of Eternal Life, foretaste of Heaven which is given to privileged souls.

This is why Joseph Francis had to live very uncommon experiences of the supernatural. Not without paying the price as we have already seen.

His life is stamped by the cross, as it has already been succintly signaled. He will have to pay the price in another way: by witnessing the essential sign Our Lady today asks of him to give to the world, her tears of reparation and supplication, for the benefit of all those who will want to take notice, and be compassionate by mingling their own sufferings and supplications. And as it always happens to those whom God has marked to transmit a sign from Heaven or a word of conversion, Joseph Francis will be contested. But let us not anticipate.

In the next pages, let us examine the forerunning signs with which Heaven prepared the Great Sign, and the privileged means that served for his own training. Later these means will be used to justify and authenticate the witness and his testimony.

Privileges or Trials?

Let us not believe that these things out of the ordinary that the witness of Our Lady bears are easy to live.

Interior locutions, ecstasies, visions of the Beyond, supernatural perceptions, commands or knowledge, dialogues with beings from Heaven, all these things, which to the eyes of the profane seem to be privileges, are they always things easy to bear?

If the spectacle of the beauties of nature elates beyond measure the one who knows how to discover within it the trace and charm of the Creator whom he then suspects as infinitely beautiful, powerful, good and tender to his creatures, and if interior contemplation follows amazement of the senses in the one who has faith, is it as easy to contemplate directly the Beyond for the one who still has his mortal body? Must the interior senses not be refined, exercised to discern that it is something really from Heaven and not an imaginative or diabolical counterfeit?

This is why suffering, a multiform and proportionate suffering, always accompanies the particular graces of this kind. And the subject is in need of a solid guide.

The Companions from Heaven

In this case the All High has seen to it by sending the Queen of prophets, the Mother of Wisdom and the first of all educators, to train his future witness and equip him against all the obstacles that would come.

For this, the Blessed Virgin does not come alone... And the lessons often take the form of a narrative of biblical events.

One day, Joseph Francis will assist to the episode of the coming of Mary and Joseph to Bethlehem for the event of the Nativity. He sees the scene unfold: the refusal, the selfishness of the inhabitants of the city of David. He is compassionate with the sorrows of the holy spouse, with his anxieties facing the impossibility of offering to the King of Heaven and earth a convenient shelter for his mortal birth. Joseph Francis *lives* the scene, and *participates* in it. And he suffers... He would like so much to be able to offer a compensation equal to his suffering. He feels his poverty, he has nothing to offer, so he thinks, and he feels distressed. The angels suggest that he offer himself...

Do we not find such sentiments and a similar answer in the life of the saints? To a privileged soul chagrined of not being able to offer anything to Our Lord, He answers her: "Give me your sins..."

Padre Pio

The Blessed Virgin does not come alone...

Joseph Francis, one day, had asked the famous stigmatized Capuchin, Padre Pio, the favor of becoming his spiritual son. Some years before the latter's death, he had begun to correspond with him and had obtained the favor he had asked. Afterwards, he often perceived at a distance the presence of his new spiritual Father. Padre Pio revealed to him one day, in a mysterious fashion, his coming death. The prophecy came about. Since, he has often appeared to Joseph Francis, and continues his protection. Joseph Francis learned one day that Padre Pio obtained a particular effective power to refrain and repel the powers of hell.

Other Celestial Protectors

Many other celestial beings, who are linked it seems with the Work of Mary for our times manifest themselves: Saint Bernard, his patron, with whom he has conversations, Saint Louis-Marie Grignion de Montfort. The angels, particularly his guardian angel, become messengers from Heaven sent to him. We already know that Padre Pio regularly used and still does use, the ministry of angels to fulfill his mission. Many of his spiritual sons have taken the habit to communicate with him through the intermediary of their guardian angel.

Mystical Life - Active Life

These manifestations of a mystical order are ordained towards something. Joseph Francis, as we have seen, saw himself engaged very early to work for the Reign of Our Lady, under the banner of her Immaculate Heart.

Now all the signs and events filling his life were to converge towards one event, and then a series of events which were to start in July 1977, and continue for more than seven years: the repeated tears of the Blessed Virgin, flowing from a statue he had gotten in a very providential way.

These events had been announced, although in a veiled manner, as is the custom with Heaven. Any prophetic announcement contains a visible part covering a hidden aspect, as a shell would an almond. In order to taste the almond, one must completely break the shell.

When the announced events come about, then the prophetical wall breaks open under the weight of these events, and the witness who bore it in silence and suffering is brought out. The prophecy become reality is now intelligible, and bears its fruits in the souls of good will.

II

Chapter 1

FORETELLING SIGNS

When the Virgin projects a visible manifestion, she often prepares the future seers or witnesses with concise facts. She will try to guard them against fear, a natural fear in front of these unusual things; or yet, to prepare their heart for the reception of a message; or for any other motive. The ways of Heaven are mysterious, and feeble is our understanding in this domain.

In Fatima, for example, the future seers of Our Lady of the Rosary had, at three different occasions, the visit of the Angel of Portugal. It was an education he obviously had to give them as he had to predispose them to receive the Virgin and Her message.

The angels being the messengers of God committed to the interests of Heaven and the service of souls, it is normal that in these cases, the Mother of God delegates them to the soul chosen to witness her solicitude.

In the present case, Joseph Francis benefits from another Kind of preparation. He was already familiar with the reality from Above. She could directly announce Herself which testimony he would be called to give; one day, the statue he would have would animate itself and transmit directly for the souls the maternal sentiments and deep anguish of the Co-Redemptrix for a world which refuses the salvation it so crucially needs.

So Mary, this time again, announces the coming miracle of another of her manifestations of mercy. She will make her witness feel, at three occasions, that one day her statue would shed tears. As with any prophetical announcement, like it is said above, it is partly visible, partly hidden.

She will send him, at intervals, two dreams, then a vision during which he will see the tears of Our Mother manifest themselves from her "image" become a "presence" of the One the image represents. In general terms, and in the broad sense of the word, is a statue not an "image", that is, the representation in three dimensions of the one whom we wish to honor? This is why the Virgin Herself will speak of her "images" that weep and express all the sentiments of Her Maternal heart. She obviously wants to speak of her "statues", although some of her images as such have also shed tears, but in an exceptional way as far as we know.

Two Foretelling Dreams

The first dream of the kind he received was given to him approximately 10 years before the first real weeping, during the night of Saturdy to Sunday, July 16, 1967.

Another dream, similar to the first one, came to him on Monday, July 17, 1972, in the evening. It seems that the month of July, a month traditionally consecrated to the Precious Blood of Our Lord, has been chosen by Mary Co-Redemptrix to make her rending call to the world.

So it was in the evening as he was then sleeping. He saw in a dream a magnificient statue start to shed tears. Her eyes were as a dam opening up to let out an abundant flow of tears.

What emotion for the poor witness, in front of such sorrow from Our Mother, so gentle, so amiable and so loved! "I then felt my heart ready to burst with pain", he says.

On many occasions, he asked the Blessed Virgin what these tears could mean. He later forgot what the answers given by Our Lady were. It was no doubt inopportune at that time to discover the reason, but only to feel the oncoming and feel the grief.

During these two dreams, prophetical messages were also given to him: the great darkness to fall down on the world, a prophecy so often announced by many prophets, the scourge of war at its paroxysm, the horrible vision of men killing each other like savage beasts, a curious sickness attacking the mind of the people, the Church decimated, and the small remnant constrained to hide underground.

A Foretelling Vision

The third announcement of her visible weepings the Virgin gave him took the form of a vision which came to him during the wee hours of a summer morning two years later.

According to the memory he has of it, it was probably on Friday, September 6, 1974. He sees this manifestation of the Blessed Virgin, not as a dream, but as an apparition, as he was then awake.

The Blessed Virgin revealed herself to him all dressed in white. It was under the well-known identity of Our Lady of Fatima that he saw her. As she was standing in front of him, she suddenly covered her face with her hands, as a person in grief and ready to weep would do. This is what in fact happened with her. She cried abundantly, her shoulders shaking with the sobs.

This lasted but a short time, then she disappeard. This is when he realized that it could not have been a dream, but really an apparition, since he had stayed awake from beginning to end.

Three years later, in July of 1977, his statue of Our Lady of Fatima acquired in the last three years from the Blue Army, would bring into concrete existence what the dreams and apparition had announced to him.

Chapter 2

ACQUISITION AND METAMORPHOSIS

The statue that weeps is a wooden statue sculptured from a block of cedar wood. Originating from Fatima, it had been sent to the Secretariat of the Blue Army of Our Lady of Fatima, in the United States, and then resold to Joseph Francis.

In May of 1974, he confides, I was at work and something "was pulling at my heart". I felt pushed to write to the Blue Army and order a statue of Our Lady of Fatima sculptured in wood. I did not have the means, but perhaps they would accept to sell it to me on credit? I also needed a crown for the statue.

The request is sent and received.

And Toni Cormier of the Center of the Blue Army answers that among all the letters received that day, she had picked up his... and what a surprise to see that the request from this correspondent could be filled immediately, a new statue mesuring 40 inches (1 meter approx.) having arrived recently at the Center from Fatima. A problem had arisen: it had to be resold very dearly. So it had been considered to return it to its point of origin. Joseph Francis' letter would change the plans. Toni made the link between Joseph Francis' request and this quite special statue, and thought that it could be sent to him. She consulted with the other people concerned, and the suggestion agreed upon.

The statue was therefore sent to Joseph Francis.

What a surprise for the latter to receive a note from the C.P.R. that a wooden crate had arrived addressed to him at the railway station.

"The crate is brought home", he says, "I succeed in opening it and on taking out the statue I am disappointed, so much so that I consider returning it."

So it seems that this "piecework" was not a total success!

It is in fact true that the statue "is not pretty at all", so thinks Joseph Francis. The "eyes are half-closed", and she looks like a person who would "have had the mumps…". He therefore decides to return it the very next day.

In the meantime, one must not show disrespect towards Our Lady, of whom this statue is "the image". So he places it on the television set and surrounds it with flowers.

During the following night, sleep does not come. Living in a small place, he is resting in the room where the statue is. All night, he twists and turns in bed.

At one point, as he has his eyes on it, something unusual happens.

He sees a red-colored ray hit the hem of Our Lady's dress, at the exact spot where there is a star fixed at the bottom of the dress. Intrigued, he sits up in his bed, in order to observe the thing.

Is it a light from the street? Impossible, the curtains are closed and too thick to let any light pierce through from outside.

Suddenly the ray disappears to give place to a sort of cloud which surrounds the statue. This cloud is luminous, and grows to the point of surrounding and hiding the statue completely. This lasts a certain time, and then the clouds slowly disappears to leave a "perfume": the air is filled with the purest scent of rose. Indeed it is a rose perfume that floats in the room.

And looking at the statue, he notices how it is changed!

It has become so beautiful! So beautiful, that he loses the idea of returning it. Moreover he now senses, besides roses, "the presence like of Heaven…"

And recalling the first impression he had of the statue, impression that had brought his decision to return it, he now regrets it and *confesses* it: "I threw myself on my knees", he says, "to ask forgiveness to Our Lord and Our Lady for having been disrespectful towards the statue."

Ravishing! Divinely Beautiful!

A ravishing beauty! Divinely beautiful! Indeed, translated in one way or the other, it is the expression of all those who have seen this statue after its unexpected transformation. The *expressions* are more or less different: the *impression* is the same.

On his first visit at Joseph Francis' place, one says: "But what a beautiful statue! Never have I seen any like it, so beautiful, live, natural…"

This observer is of a certain age, a practicing catholic having visited a quantity of churches and pilgrim places, and thus brought to admire many works of all styles and all epochs. His cry of admiration has a value corresponding to the numerous experiences he has lived.

"It has a particularly live countenance", say the numerous people who have been able to admire it.

"I got close to admire her better", says one of them. "Her eyes mostly attracted me... I looked, expécting that at any moment they would blink, as the statue gave so much the impression to be alive."

"What a ravishing beauty! I did not want to speak loudly, for I had the impression I was in church. We could feel an atmosphere which is beyond anything we can imagine."

"Her cheeks seemed so smooth that I asked Joseph Francis permission to touch them... It is certainly not an ordinary statue."

"What a beautiful statue! It has the most beautiful face of the Blessed Virgin that I have ever seen", says another.

"The sight of the beautiful dear Mother of Fatima dazzled me so much that I could not say one word all the time our visit lasted", recounts one person who had the privilege to go and pray at the feet of this Pilgrim statue.

A priest in turn gives his testimonial: "The first thing that I noticed with this statue that I had never seen was its great beauty..."

And another person, at whose home the Pilgrim statue made a halt for a month, narrates how it had seemed alive and expressive. Its countenance changed from the greatest sorrow to serenity and joy at the welcome she received at her place, following the rejection she had received at another place. And she seemed to scrutinize closely this faithful soul who loves her so much. The latter did not feel perturbed: do we feel disturbed with so good a Mother who only seeks to guess our needs the better to satisfy them?

There is no doubt that the Virgin has put in this image of herself which she has remodeled, a spark of her Divine beauty, and that what makes it vibrate with so much intensity is her own Immaculate Heart, so tender, so merciful, so loving for her children of the earth so sick today, so sick, so wanting!

Chapter 3

THE FIRST WEEPING

It is this magnificent statue, remodeled it seems through the care of Our Lady herself, that started to shed tears on a certain day of July in 1977...

Here is how Joseph Francis relates the event.

"It was in 1977, on the 29th of July, which was the last Friday of the month, around 5 o'clock in the afternoon. I had just come back from a few errands. As it was a beautiful day, with a very hot sun and a sky as blue as it could be, I had walked back.

"Upon arrival I fell in the same armchair which is still there, facing directly the statue of Our Lady - this was told in 1982 - and I sat thinking..."

"The week before, I had talked to Our Lady about my financial problems: delay in paying the bills for want of money... and then I forgot it all."

His reflection then went backwards a couple of months. He had one day proposed to his brother to take some photos of the beautiful statue, adorned by an appropriate decor by taking it outside in the midst of trees and flowers. These photos would be offered, without fixing a price, but yet asking for a free offering, to Catholic magazines in order to help spread the message of Fatima. The offerings would be to cover the costs only, no profit being sought from this operation, but only the reimbursement of the expenses.

"I could this way", he continues, "have enough candles and also the oil that I must now have following the desire of Our Lady."

At the time he is relating this, five years later, no photos had yet been sold: all had been given...

Joseph Francis is now sitting in front of Our Lady, tired from the day, fatigued from the burden of financial difficulties.

He is not complaining. He is telling his fatigue, and mainly his deception of not being able to do more for the reign of the Immaculate Heart of Mary.

11

1984

My eyes flow without ceasing.

(Lam. 3, 49)

12 October 1984

Bitterly she weeps at night, tears upon her cheeks,
With not one to console her of all her dear ones...

(Lam. 1, 2)

October 1984

Come, all you Who pass by the way look and see
whether there is any suffering like my suffering.

(Lam. 1, 16)

14

October 1984

"Are you not aware of how I am... pleading?"

(Message to Don Gobbi, 21/1/1978)

15   October 1984

There with thee to weep and pray, is all
I ask of thee to give.

(Stabat Mater)

16   October 1984
"… I ask you all to heed my anguished appeal."
(Message to Don Gobbi, 21/1/1978)

17   October 27, 1984
"O Mary! Queen of Martyrs, Pray for us!"

18   October 27, 1984

"There are so many who do not know me!"

(Message of La Salette)

For his life, of which we have only unveiled but a small corner, is totally consecrated to the Reign of the Immaculate Heart of Mary and that of Her Son.

And it is then, at that precise moment, when he came kneeling at the feet of her statue, that the first tears appear and fall on the forehead of the faithful witness.

It is 5 o'clock in the afternoon, a Friday in July, a month traditionally consecrated to the devotion of the Precious Blood of Christ, Blood shed for the Redemption of the world...

The First Tear

It is at this moment, when Joseph Francis is kneeling at the feet of the beautiful Madonna, and praying with all his heart, that the first tear flows and falls on his forehead.

He is far from imagining what is happening at that moment. He thinks of the roof which has already leaked, and again could...

"Oh no! Not again! Is the roof leaking again?"

"But no! The roof cannot leak with a beautiful July sun, and not the smallest cloud in the sky!

He casts a look outside and notices that it is as nice as before.

Raising his eyes towards the beautiful Madonna, he notices that the eyes are imbued with what seems to be tears.

And the shock came!

How not to be profoundly upset when one is called Joseph Francis, loving Our Lady so much, praying in front of such a beautiful statue of the Blessed Virgin and suddenly seeing tears appear in her eyes!

"I felt a shock", he says. Never shall I forget it. Tears - or something liquid - filled the eyes of the statue. I was stupefied!

He got up, not knowing what to think, say or do.

"So many things went through my mind at the time", he adds. It would have been astonishing otherwise!

How did he get the idea to go and fetch his camera to photograph?

A sudden impression? An interior locution?

"Something told me: 'Go and get your camera!'"

He had in the house a film and some flashcubes.

The statue was then surrounded by a circling light, not perceptible to the eye, but able to impress the film, and he will have the proof after the film is developed.

So he gets ready to take photos of the Virgin weeping through her statue.

The Presence of God?

At the take of the first photo, he says, this light which surrounded the statue threw him backwards with so much force that he was projected against a small table standing at the other side of the room, without however suffering the least hurt at the moment of the brutal contact.

He wanted to take a second photo. Again at the take of the snapshot, he was projected, this time towards the door. As it is open, it is against the screen door he will rebound. This time again, he does not feel any pain.

This force is powerful, invincible, but not malevolent. He does not really know how to explain it, but what he knows is that it is linked to the mysterious light which bathes the statue at the time of the tears.

(If I may here open an interrogative parenthesis, this light doubled with a force, could it be this mysterious "presence of God" he had felt on many occasions since his childhood, and that one day made the shack in which he was praying shake? Could it be also this "mysterious presence", at the same time light and power, which scared the prophets of the Old Testament and incited the men of the time to turn away the face in order not to see the "Glory of God"?

If the answer to this question is affirmative, this mysterious presence of God, could we think that it is today less terrifying from the fact that we are in the era of salvation and that God now shows himself to us under the mantle of mercy merited for us by His Son?

Besides, this presence of God carried by the all gentle, all tender and commiserate Mother could it remain terrifying?)

At the take of the third photo, he does not undergo the same effect of the force, although the light is still there.

"I felt that this time, it was different", he says. There was no more any force which pushed. The light still continued to swirl around the statue in tears. But how powerful was this force! I do not really know how to describe it.

From that day on, he continues to see the light around the statue when it weeps; he does not feel the effect of its energy anymore".

A Mysterious Light

Praying, he took other photos, with a contrite and grieved heart, and the fear of having committed some fault which was afflicting the Heart of the Mother and that of the Son. Our Lord was permitting this to happen to draw his attention.

So he prayed, asking forgiveness in case these tears had meant the need to repent.

Or else, could it be a "trick" of the Devil? The question quickly went through his mind. He prayed too to be enlightened and, need be, to repulse the Wicked One.

We shall see later that this phenomenon could not come from hell, as Joseph Francis had suffered, a few months before, an infernal violence directed after all against the statue and the One it represents.

So he took pictures... And they were extraordinary!

The light which he perceived, since the transformation of the statue, and which now manifests itself at the time of the tears, is like a cloud, a sort of cloud of light which swirls around the statue and thus provides the luminosity necessary for the snapshots. Or which, in any case, is sufficiently perceptible to influence the film.

This phenomenon was noticed by the photographers who developed the photos.

"These first photos", says Joseph Francis, "showed like a swirl of light of the colors of the rainbow surrounding the statue, to the point of hiding it. It is this kind of phenomenon which had occurred on the night when the statue had transformed and embellished itself.

This whirl of light of the colors of the rainbow was visible on the first pictures, and so unusual was it that those who had to develop the film were greatly astonished.

"They took the trouble to telephone me" says Joseph Francis, "to tell me that there was "something strange" with my camera!

An Improvised Oratory

Let us again go over the complex impressions lived by Joseph Francis that day.

First, there is a reaction of fear, asking himself if he had sinned in some way against Our Lord and Our Lady.

A prayer both compassionate and contrite.

A prudent prayer destined to chase away any demoniac influence, in case there was.

And then, to crown his prayer, an attitude of abandonment, of disponibility and humility.

Was it necessary to speak about that? Perhaps. But to whom? And how? And through what channel? Joseph Francis is poor, deprived of any means of action.

ON ONE HAND, he definitely felt that this manifestation of the Mother of God was destined to **the people of God,** and that he had to pass on what he received.

At the time of his narration on tape, he said this: "I want to talk here about what happened after the statue of Our Lady of Fatima started to weep, this statue of which I am only the guardian, for it does not belong to me in fact. It belongs to the people of God, not only in Canada, but of the whole world..."

And further in the same narration: "I do not feel any shame in front of the tears of the Virgin, which have often been tears of joy. And I think about all those who have been able to see it. Everything is in God's hands now, and I am grateful to Him. He has the right to all praises. And so, if anyone receives any graces through this story, it is all I ask."

ON THE OTHER HAND, there is a need for discretion, a reserve I would say natural that experience the mystics in front of these manifestations of Heaven and which inclines them to hide in their heart the "secret of the King". "And his mother kept all these words in her heart." (Luke 2, 51)

He also asked himself what kind of reception would be made to such revelations...

Not knowing too much how to come out of this dilemma, Joseph Francis relied on God Himself for the follow-up it was necessary to give to this matter.

"For a good while", he says, "I was afraid of speaking of it to anyone. Who would understand that a statue is weeping, as I myself have difficulty in realizing it?" I asked myself. "It then came to my mind that if I did not speak about it, God Himself would take charge of it in his time."

And that is what He did.

One day, some visitors were attracted, one does not really know how, and they find themselves in front of the Madonna, during his absence. This is how it came about. A lady he well knew, with one of her friends, had gone to the beach with the children for summer swimming. On their way back, they all stop at Joseph Francis' place, who is absent, and prayer it is in front of the beautiful statue in tears...

Back at his place, he is very surprised to see the room filled with people, adults and children, gazing and praying to Our Lady in tears.

One of these people confides that she has prayed to be delivered from the need of drinking.

It was one of the ways God used to make known the message of the Virgin in tears.

One can suppose that this kind of experience did not stay without an echo, and the information quickly spread throughout the neighborhood.

The statue cried anew, again and again, drawing witnesses in growing numbers. The first summer, from the end of July to the end of September, over eight hundred people witness the tears of Our Lady.

The news traveled in the family in a natural way, without the witness having to do anything to draw the attention. During a visit to one of his sisters, the latter noticed something unusual about him. Between brother and sister, confidence is easy, and soon she was able to admire the beautiful pictures. In turn she finds herself in prayer in front of the afflicted Madonna, bringing other people.

In February of the following year, a priest whom Joseph Francis knows well comes to the knowledge of these marvellous events. He comes accompanied by a teacher. On his second visit, he brings a camera, and the photos will come out very beautiful. Later he goes to Toronto where he related the story of the weeping statue, and leaves some photos. These will trace the way which the Pilgrim Virgin will later follow.

Chapter 4

DIABOLICAL ASSAULT

As soon as the Virgin sets her foot somewhere on the globe, the infernal Dragon intervenes, trying by all means to wreck the action of mercy she has the mission to accomplish. The apparitions or manifestations of Mary are ordinarily, either preceded or followed by tactics of diversions, or followed by persecution.

Let us think of the false apparitions which took place in Lourdes, of the violent or underhanded persecutions which befell the shepherds of La Salette and those of Fatima. Let us think of the silence which envelops a number of Marian manifestations which, even though are not authenticated by the Church, remain no less trustworthy because of the signs that accompany them. Diversion, violence, silence, anything is good and useful to the adversary of Our Lady.

Would Satan allow the Virgin to undertake another action of mercy, this time under the traits of a pilgrim statue that weeps, without intervening?

God permits him to take action while giving the witness the graces he then needs. Joseph Francis indeed, one day, came under a diabolical attack obviolsy aimed at making the statue disappear and to repeal the graces which, through it, were destined to the Church and humanity.

This happened towards the end of the fall of 1976, about six or seven months before the event of the first weeping.

A Terrible Presence...

Joseph Francis had lain down on his bed towards the end of the afternoon, wanting to get some rest before going out in the evening as planned to a prayer meeting.

"As I did not want to miss the mass which would be said at the meeting, I did want to attend."

"All of a sudden", he says, "I felt a terrible presence in my bedroom... and a malefic odor, like that of a filthy stench from a sewer, even worse, as I had never ever smelled the like in all my life."

"I tried to turn around", he adds, "feeling that something was close to my cot. As I could not turn, I tried then to turn my head to see what it was. I could feel a coldness run over me. Oh! how cold it was, I do remember!

These diabolical manifestations are often accompanied by these sewer stenches, and this unexplainable glacial cold which penetrates and provokes an uneasiness, a profound distaste, at the same time physical, mental and spiritual. It is something undefinable. The authors who have studied these diabolical phenomena unanimously speak about these sensations and this glacial coldness.

It was obviously the Devil.

"And suddenly, I heard this horrible voice which said: 'I want you to see these things.' "

"And there in front of me", adds Joseph Francis, "I saw all kinds of beautiful clothes, diamonds, rings, like I had never seen, mounted with precious stones... big and small diamonds. Besides that, I could have many mansions... I counted four."

At this point of the narrative, how can one not think of the triple temptation of Our Lord? Satan is always the same. How would he have liked to wreck the mission of the Redeemer. He submitted Christ to the three temptations corresponding to the three human weaknesses which resulted from the original sin: the three concupiscences. And Our Lord was willing to submit to temptation in order to teach us how to resist and obtain for us the necessary graces.

All men, in diverse degrees and under one form or the other, are led into temptation. Particularly those who are called to a particular mission in the Church, or who have a special or important function.

A Deal...

Satan knew without doubt the power which had been associated with the miraculous statue for the salvation of souls, what graces would flow with the tears falling from the eyes of Our Lady, and what role, as a witness and messenger, would play the proprietor of this statue.

He therefore wanted to get rid of the statue, and at the same time annul the vocation of the one who up to this day had been its guardian.

"At this point", says Joseph Francis, "I could not know whether it was Satan, Lucifer or one of his demons. At least I knew I was not possessed."

In fact, from what he tells us, during all this assault, never did he lose control of his senses, or the full consciousness of what was going on and what was the stake of the battle. The attack came from outside and did not reach him in his soul or faculties.

Satan continued: "I will give you all that..."

And he showed him scenes of carnal pleasures, along with others of wealth. He promised that he would become rich if he consented to his proposition.

"I became afraid when he told me that, as I could see all what he was showing me, but", affirms Joseph Francis, "I opposed him with a..."

"No!"

"He still continued to show me other desirable things: cars - I could not even drive - and all the worldly glory I could wish..."

There was in the offer of Satan a serious question mark. Satan was promising all these "desirable" things as seen under the satanic angle and outside the salvation path, but he did not say for how many years he could enjoy them.

"For a number of years" recalls Joseph Francis, "but he did not say how many..."

It is therefore a bargain that was proposed to him: But what in return? Would Joseph Francis have to consent or sacrifice?

"In return, I had to permit him to take my will, let him guide me, but at the cost of my soul, in the end."

What a terrible deal!

And Joseph Francis quickly understook what was at stake at the bottom of this satanic errand. Lucifer wants souls; he takes them by assaulting one by one and would not leave one outside his power if it were permitted and possible for him. But here, on that day, it was not mainly Joseph Francis' soul which he desired. Through the disciple, he wanted to take over the statue in order to neutralize it.

And talking about the statue, Satan made sure not to mention the name of "Mary", or any other of the vocables of the Blessed Virgin, as this is not permitted to him. And he is incapable of doing so, as the name of "Mary" carries in itself a capacity of salvation.

MARY! The evocation of this sublime name is a grace, a call to Redemption.There is total incompatibility between the gentle name of the Virgin and the perverse breath of the Adversary of God.

Talking about Our Lady, present under the traits of the statue, he would only say these words: "that statue, there!"

And it was that wooden carved statue of Our Lady of Fatima whose tears would soon gush out in nearly uninterrupted outpourings, which he wanted to eliminate.

In the Name of Jesus and Mary...

Possessed by grace and Our Lady, Joseph Francis did not let Satan possess him.

"No", he cried out, "I prefer to be poor in goods, but rich in the graces of God. You have nothing to do with me, Satan. In the name of Jesus Christ, by the Very Precious Blood which has saved our souls, Satan, He has won the battle. You, you are but a loser, a liar. If you are he or one of his adepts, I rebuke you in the precious name of Mary, the Blessed Virgin, and in the Name of the Holy Heart of Jesus, go back to hell and leave these premises, leave this house which belongs to God. You are here in a holy place."

This exorcism was too much for the infernal intruder. He had to renounce to his project, and before leaving frothed his violent but useless rage.

"Then", says the witness of Our Lady, "he starded to curse, swear and howl, as I have never heard in all my life. I was horrified. I had seen the movie 'The Exorcist', but it was nothing in comparison to what I could see and hear."

"He said to me: 'You will be a failure. I will damn you.'"

Joseph Francis answers: "You will not touch me, for I belong to God. I belong to Mary and Jesus, the Lamb of the Precious Blood. By the cross we are saved. Jesus has won the battle: we are free to go home, and your promises and the rest of your things are but worldly things. I do not want any if it means denying my Lord and my Lady."

And it was the breaking loose of the satanic rage against poor Joseph Francis, and the furious madness against anything he could seize. His room was ransacked and the poor occupant mistreated.

"He howled" says Joseph Francis, "and started throwing things around, even though the room was too small to throw things any distance. He overturned the cot, throwing down the lamp. He howled again, and then, the more I mentioned the names of Jesus and Mary, the more he let go at me with piercing screams. And all started to fly in the room. He threw down my bookcase over my bed already upside-down. I saw myself being covered with contusions, which I only felt afterwards."

Joseph Francis noticed that the Demon did not at any moment look towards the statue. Having to pass in front of it on the way out, he kept his back turned. The curtain parted at the passage of the infernal spirit, but Joseph Francis did not see the front door open. The tempter went out raging his vexation.

This assault left the faithful servant of Our Lady covered with bruises, and his home in a mess.

"Still unable to gather my wits", he says, "and trembling with fear I looked at the statue and stammered something on my way to the bathroom."

"It is then I became aware of the injuries all over me. I started to clean them with a cloth and as I wiped them they disappeared together with the hurt."

"I know all this seems implausible and incredible, but it is the plain truth."

Chapter 5

SEVEN YEARS OF WEEPING

(A) An Animated Statue

Is it surprising to learn that this magnificent statue is the result of a very particular operation by the Virgin? She wanted to improve the work of the artist. A sculptor, however competent, pious and devoted he is to interest of religion, can he adequately express what is Divine?

Seers search for words, or expressions susceptible of expressing the inexpressible. How to represent the Mother of God, divinely beautiful, pure reflection of the Divinity? God it is said, exhausted his creative power in creating the Mother of His Son. Therefore, how can the most skilful, the most competent, the most believing - since these are created in faith - artist come close to such a sublime Reality?

And Mary wants today to effectively touch the rebel heart of man, astounded by his own techniques to the point of forgetting or rejecting the eternal realities. So she offers to his eyes and his other senses something capable of really moving him: the reflection of her Divine beauty, and the fragance of her virtues, with the sorrow of her tears.

Lucy of Fatima tells us:

It is "impossible to describe her as she really is..." (1)

How "to paint the light and the beauty which adorned her?"

Melanie, shepherdess of La Salette, had given us the following portrait:

"The Blessed Virgin was all beautiful and formed of love; looking at her, I longed to become one with her. In her fineries as in her person, everything breathed the majesty, the splendor, the magnificence of an incomparable Queen. She looked beautiful, white, immaculate, crystallized, dazzling, celestial, fresh...; it seemed that the word "Love" escaped from her silver and all pure lips. She seemed to me like a good Mother, full of goodness, amiability, love for us, compassion, and mercy." (2)

It is something of this inexpressible beauty, as much by words as by the brush or the chisel of the artist, that Our Lady has wanted to recreate in the statue that Joseph Francis had acquired in the spring of 1974. This magnificence was first meant for him to satisfy to the full his eyes and heart, to stir up his love, to nourish his fidelity and fortify his engagement. And, later, the Divine image of Mary would cry, and through her tears, would attract to her the souls of good will.

Our Lady of Akita

Does this very particular solicitude astonish?

To my knowledge, She has already manifested it at least one other time. And it was in Japan, a few years before the similar event here in Canada.

There also, the Virgin has modified the image of herself that was venerated.

In a booklet which has just been published, Fr. Shimura Tatsuya, Curate and administrator of the Cathedral of Tokyo, reports the fact of the metamorphosis of the Statue of Akita, which also sheds tears.

"The statue, carved in wood and 70 cm. (28 in.) tall, represents the Virgin who is standing on the globe, in front of a cross. To their astonishment, the Sisters noticed one day that the expression of her countenance had changed."

"Around mid-September 1974, the sculptor, Mr. Saburo Wakasa (Member of the Japanese Institute of Sculpture), was called and here is his testimony: 'As soon as I saw the statue again, two things struck me: the cheeks that I had hollowed out had sunk, the countenance had refined itself; on the other hand, the color of the face had turned to a dark chestnut. I remember having found the expression more penetrating, no doubt because of the change at the level of the cheeks.'" (3)

That the statue recently acquired by Joseph Francis had one evening changed itself, to become the exquisite Madonna we never tire of contemplating, and which brings us closer to God, is a fact that was not therefore unique.

All the epithets expressing beauty, magnificence, esthetics, splendor, grace, are found on the lips of those who have been able to admire it, either immobile, or at the moments when the Virgin expressed herself through her representation. I have already said a word on this splendor; I shall add here a few words on the life, the expressions which exudes from it, by borrowing from the testimonials of those who have seen...

"Its eyes", says one, "were of great beauty but sad, and its countenance expressed sorrow."

"She has something particular, profound, live, natural", says another.

"The characteristic trait of this beauty is its livingness."

"The statue gives the impression that we are in the presence of a living person, and what a person!"

"The countenance goes through the expressions a human countenance can take."

In one of the messages to Don Stefano Gobbi, of which I have already spoken before, Our Lady had announced that she was expressing herself through her statues:

"As a Mother I wish to speak to you, I who am here with you, represented by the statue you have here. Every statue of mine is a sign of my presence, and reminds you of your heavenly Mother. Therefore each of them should be honored..."

"A sign also of how much I like the fitting veneration given to my images is what I am effecting through this little statue. It is a triple sign I give you: that of my eyes, which suddenly come alive; that of the color of my countenance, which changes its hue; and that of my Heart, which exudes a fragrance, now a delicate one, now one of greater strength." (4)

What the Mother of God operates generally in a more or less perceptible fashion, why could she not in a flashing and privileged way, through a statue that she herself has metamorphosed, making it apt to communicate her most live sentiments?

The Garment

The varied manifestations of the sentiments expressed through the hue of the countenance and by her expression, some have noticed them also at the level of the garment of the Madonna.

For example, at certain moments, the mantle of the Virgin has changed color.

One day, a priest very devoted to her, having preached on the devotion of the Blessed Virgin and the Marian Movement, saw the color of the Madonna's mantle change, taking on one of his favorite colors. Did the Blessed Virgin not want to show him how much she appreciated his Marian apostolate and his devotion to Her cause?

Saint Thomas Aquinas, in front of the Blessed Sacrament, heard one day Our Lord tell him: *"You have spoken well of Me"*. To her beloved son, did Our Lady not want, in "coloring" her garment with one of his favorite colors, translate the same thought: *"My son, you have spoken well of Me?"*

(B) She Cries with Us and over Us

This statue has wept for over seven years.

Or rather, our Heavenly Mother, through her statue.

How not to be moved to mingle our own tears to those of the Blessed Virgin, at this solemn and tragic instant in the destiny of humanity!

Frequency

In the third part of this book you will be able to read the circumstanced narration of many weepings noticed by some ten-scores of people, from whom a testimonial has been obtained. Hundreds of others could be added.

From July 29, 1977 onwards, the miraculous statue has shed tears on a regular basis; we could say daily, without exaggerating. Up to three hundred weepings a year, actually meaning six days a week on the average.

The witness has not noted each of the events. The thing was impossible to him because of the frequency and the length of the phenomenon, on account also of the dialogues which, on a daily basis, repeat themselves, accompanying or preceding the manifestations of the tears.

These weepings come about in a varied way. Often, only a few tears will flow. They are a sign of joy, for the reception by a new follower who will become a witness to her requests and a messenger of her pleas for prayer and conversion.

At other moments, the tears will be more abundant and will repeat themselves intermittently during the same day. In fact this relates to a single weeping prolonging itself in varied intensity, hot tears followed by a moment of rest as it happens when one is shaken by a heavy grief.

The tears flow out more frequently at the end of the day, or in the evening.

... with Us

These afflictions are related to distressing events which happen in the world or which touch the Church. The approach of grave events, war, revolutions, social unrests, earthquakes and cataclysms, corruption of the world, division among the followers of Her Son, the abandonment of her children, the contempt she suffers on the part of many of her sons: these are all causes for the affliction of the Immaculate Heart of Mary whose tears bear witness.

Thus at the time of the criminal attempt against the Holy Father, in May of 1981, the Virgin cried intensely. One day, her messenger was prejudiced against. She was profoundly afflicted by it, and her tears fell in torrents.

The Mother of the Church suffers with her children. She suffers because of them, but also, she cries with them when they undergo trials. She affirms this in the message to Don Gobbi, that I have already quoted:

"By the sign I give you in the color of my visage, I want to show you that I am a Mother for all, and today I share in all your needs, and I rejoice in all your joys. But I also suffer in all your numerous sufferings."

"When you suffer, I suffer. When you rejoice, I rejoice..."

"Look at my merciful eyes which shed tears of sorrow and compassion. In so many parts of the world I give this sign, causing copious tears to stream from my eyes, even tears of blood." (1)

Hence, Mary cries for us; she cries over us; and she cries with us.

There is not one sorrowful event happening at any point on this planet that does not distress her. And her tears fall, silent and abundant, but so sorrowful to the heart of those who have had the privilege to see them flow.

... but Also of Joy!

If the tears express sadness, sorrow, most often, they can also indicate joy. The Virgin does not miss the occasion to show her sentiments of joy, by letting a few tears bead, the sight of which will incline to serenity rather than to compassion.

To this one, she will thus say that she is happy to see him run to her bidding and that his fidelity touches her heart directly. Such tears of joy are often accompanied by a fragrance which will express more vividly the sentiment she wants to manifest.

At another time, she will cry for joy in seeing assembled around her statue souls who will have to play a role in passing on her messages: through collaboration, testimony, mutual support.

One day, the statue having been profaned, a lady receives her with joy in her home. Very happy to see her solitude filled by such a beautiful Madonna, she was praying with fervor when the statue let flow a few tears. Later came the confirmation that Our Lady had shed tears of joy, as had seen the faithful hostess of Our Lady.

... and over Us

But again, where to look for the ultimate cause of this uninterrupted flow of tears, the cause of a countenance broken with sorrow and so soul wrenching? This question poses another question.

Why does a mother cry, if not because her children are in danger? or because they are ingrate and do not follow the way shown by the father? The mother of God, seeing humanity today far from the roads of salvation, and noticing that the Church of Her Son, itself, needs straightening, would she be more unfeeling than a mother on earth?

Is it necessary to go into details? The testimonials of many which will follow will help us to precise this: a loving son, a faithful and docile daughter do understand these things quickly.

The Need of Consolation and Cooperation

Would the Mother of God not be in need, she also, of consolation? Would she not suffer from the lack of cooperation on the part of those she has called to help her realize her plan?

I referred before to another statue which weeps in another part of the earth, over there, far away, in the same hemisphere as ours: in Akita, Japan.

One day, an angel appeared to the confidante to tell precisely the reason for the tears of the Blessed Virgin:

"Do not be astonished to see the Virgin cry. One single soul that converts and consecrates itself to God is precious to her Heart. She manifests her sorrow to stir up your faith, so inclined to weaken. Now that you have seen her tears, to console her, talk about it with courage, spread this devotion for her glory and that of Her Son. (2)

The witnesses to the tears of Our Lady thus have therefore the precise task to make known to others these manifestations of mercy from the Mother of Mercy.

An Immense Sorrow

If the weepings are varied in frequency and duration, they also vary in intensity.

Sometimes the tears are sparse, they flow slowly, and the phenomenon lasts but a short ime. At other times, there will be an abundance. A sort of swelling shows around the eyes, bursts and the tears run, abundant, down the

19

October 25, 1984

*"Never as in the present time has your heavenly
Mother been so concerned and anguished."*

(Message to Don Gobbi, 21/1/1978)

October 1984

My eyes are dimmed with sorrow.

(Ps. 6, 8)

21   November 5, 1984
Listen, all you peoples and behold my suffering.
                                  (Lam. 1, 18)

22   November 1984
"And now my sorrow bursts forth as a flooding river
bursts through all its embankments."
(Message to Don Gobbi, 13/4/1979)

23   November 1984
"I would have liked to throw myself in her arms and say:
'My good Mother, do not cry!'"
(Mélanie, of La Salette)

24   November 5, 1984
"I would have liked to console her,
so she would not cry anymore..."
                                        (Mélanie, of La Salette)

25   November 11, 1984

"Help me, my beloved sons..."

(Message to Don Gobbi, 21/1/78)

26   November 14, 1984
"Since the time that I suffer for you."
                              (Mélanie, of La Salette)

cheeks, and gather under the chin as is shown in many pictures, and fall at the feet of the statue.

In between these two examples, all the possible degrees occur. This suggests a continuous sorrow and sadness, at the same time human and out of the ordinary.

When a human being is shaken by great grief, the intensity of the tears vary according to the fatigue and the violence of the emotion. The "hot tears" and the sobs are interrupted by more or less long intervals. So it is with the weeping Virgin.

Are we not witnessing the expression of the deep sorrow of The One, who while being human is capable of our emotion and our tears, and who is, at the same time, apt to assume an immeasurable burden since she is, by her prerogatives, at the frontiers of the created and the Divine?

The Virgin who weeps, is she not the Co-Redemptrix exhaling from her Sorrowful and Immaculate Heart the extreme desolation to which she is reduced by the spectacle of the corruption of the world, the malice of man, the indifference of too great a number of her children, the treachery of those she had called and who now are in league with her Adversary?

O Mother More Than Good!

In reading the moving testimonials of those who have seen Our Lady cry and who have shed tears with Her, I feel I am brought back to this other testimony that is both a prayer and an homage to Mary Co-Redemptrix.

And an engagement!

Who else besides Melanie, the shepherdess of La Salette, can best express, in condensed form, the sentiments of compassion which must feel the real sons and daughters of Mary, in front of the sorrow of our Mother?

With the narrative of her experience, she wrote:

"The tears of our tender Mother, far from lessening her majestic and Queenly deportment, seemed on the contrary to enhance her, to make her more loveable, more beautiful, more powerful, more full of love, more maternal, more ravishing! And I would have eaten her tears which made my heart jump with compassion and love."

"To see my Mother cry, and such a Mother, without imagining some way to console her, to change her sorrows to joy, can it be understood?

"O Mother more than good!" (3)

To Awaken and Revive Our Faith

A cenacle (prayer meeting) of the Marian Movement is held in the presence of the Statue in tears. It is shedding tears while also giving forth her fragrance. The persons present will be able to testify, and the graces received with the inhaled scent will contribute to fortify the spiritual engagement and promote the devotion to the Immaculate Heart of Mary.

Is anyone sceptical? The perception of the fragrance will give him the evidence which his heart needs to establish itself firmly in the belief of the live presence of our Mother near us.

For, what it is really all about is a matter of: FAITH

The statues are images: the exterior signs are just there to be a representation, sometimes an evidence, of the presence of God, of His Mother, or some celestial messengers. There is no more faith! Mary, very merciful, animates her "images". What a responsibility it would be for us not to take notice!

If it is improper to pass without stopping in front of a statue of Our Lady, what is graver is that this coldness could be a sign of an absence of faith or love. We are touching here to something fundamental: the signal value of this gift, the invaluable gift that God gives to the modern world, to render perceptible what stems from faith: the presence on earth of His Mother who became our Mother on Golgotha. But then! what will become of the one who makes himself "capable" and "culpable" of seeing nothing and remain like a block of marble in front of such mercy!

(C) The Language of the Virginal Fragrance

Wanting to draw to her the soul of her sinful and distracted children, to direct them afterwards towards her Son, why would the Blessed Virgin not make them "taste" the sweetness of her virginal fragrance?

You will forgive me to seemingly rationalize, or render necessary what depends on the most evident mercy. God is not obliged... to go that far to urge the good will of the lost lamb. But his mercy is without limits! Humanity is today so far from the road of salvation that God will resort to unique means to attract it to Him.

Before for the Redemption, He sent his only Son. Today it seems that the Son is not sufficient; God delegates His Mother.

And so for the past one hundred and fifty years, Our Lady travels the roads of the world, transmitting the Father's call of mercy to the rebel and ingrate generations, sons of the Revolution, that the modern world secretes.

And this is not yet enough. So Mary will therefore send out a

LAST CALL

God draws yet more from the infinite treasures of His Mercy. And Mary, through her animated statues, is multiplying herself around the globe, crying, consoling, encouraging her children, attempting by all kinds of ways to open their heart to God and Her Son.

And as man today does not like sermons - who goes to hear sermons today? are there still any sermons? - Our Lady will draw them to Her as one draws children: *by appealing to their senses.*

While shedding tears, She communicates to them the fragrance of her virtues, and will manifest the celestial beauty of her countenance of the Mother of God.

And while opening our nostrils to the celestial fragrances of the most pure Virgin, why not open at the same time our heart to the spiritual marvels these perfumes express. The bee, attracted by the aroma of flowers, settles down on them to extract the nectar that will serve as food in the beehive. And the honey will rejoice the palate of man. The soul, attracted by the celestial fragrances that Mary spreads on earth, will find in Her Son's Church the food it greatly needs on the road to Eternity.

Saint Joseph, a Witness

"I untie my tongue to defend the virginal purity of my Spouse Mary, who was given to me by God. (...)

"I protected her jealously, as one can preserve a precious and delicate pearl of great value." (...)

"I had no fear to be chosen Her Spouse, for on approaching her, I inhaled the interior fragrance which exuded from her Purity and inunded my soul with a chaste joy." (1)

There seems to be a tradition in the earthly manifestations of this fragrance of Our Lady, of which Saint Joseph was the first and the most perfect beneficiary.

Our Lady of Puy

Hence, at Our Lady of Puy (5th century), the holy bishop Vosy, answering a request formulated for two centuries by the Mother of God herself, decided to build the first sanctuary at that place. He obtained through the Sovereign Pontiff the services of a pious architect and the temple was soon ready for the dedication. On his way to Rome to solicit permission to consecrate it and secure some relics for it, these are given to him at a crossroad by some mysterious persons who advise the two travelers to return to the sanctuary, that the permission was given and that everything was ready for the ceremony.

On nearing the sanctuary, they are astounded to see that the feast had already begun, a magnificent light shining through the stained windows, angelic hymns heard and celestial perfumes exuding from the sanctuary. The dedication of the chapel had been handed to the angels, and so it was called afterwards: *"The Angelic Chamber."* (2)

Our Lady of Laus

This sanctuary is reputed particularly for the fragrances the Virgin spread not only in the sanctuary but in the countryside as well.

"To the instant cure of the most varied sicknesses, writes an author, the Virgin was pleased to add yet another very special privilege: the fragrances of Laus."

"That is odors of wholly celestial charm and so intense that from the holy place which was the center, they spread to the entire valley. All the people of the time talked about it with admiration."

"The odors of Mary, it was written, are so suave, so delicate and give such a great consolation that the one who scents them believes enjoying an aforetaste of heaven. As they strike the olfactory sense they elevate the soul and all its powers and fill the heart with joy. The fragrances of flowers are nothing in comparison to these as they are effusions from the DIVINITY." (3)

Fatima

The chronicle of the Fatima apparitions tells us a fact, charming in naïveté but precious in regard to the spiritual effect the fragrance can produce on souls.

Following the suppressed apparition of August 13, the children have the joy to see the Blessed Virgin in Valinhos. She sets her feet on the branches of a green oak, like the ones in great number in that place. This is why the children feel free to cut and take the branches with them.

Lucy's mother refuses to believe in the apparition.

"But yes!", answers Jacinth, "we have seen her! Look, aunt, She had a foot on this branch and the other on that one."

"Liars!... let me see."

And Maria-Rosa takes a branch in her hand. At once all those present smell a delicious fragrance of an unknown essence coming from the dark green foliage.

This phenomenon strongly impressed Lucy's mother who from now on began to admit the hypothesis that her daughter could be telling the truth. She was already shaken by the narrative of the extraordinary phenomena noticed by so many witnesses at the Cova da Iria, six days earlier. (4)

The Mystical Rose

At Malines-sur-Meuse, in Belgium, a statue of Mary, the Mystical Rose has been shedding tears since August 8, 1983. In a recently published booklet, Fr. Gerhard Hermes, S.A.C., publisher and chief editor of the review "Der Fels", reports the fact and points out that his incredulity towards the fragrance of the Virgin was definitely vanquished by his personal perception of the fact. He writes:

"And to say that not so long ago, I had secretly smiled on hearing a confrere talk about the scent of rose coming from the tears of the "Mystical Rose", maliciously mistrusting his sense of smell! And now I myself experience the sensation: the few ends of tissue given to me and that I carry in a pocket of my coat, near the heart, give out continually, like an enveloping cloud, the scent equivalent to that of a whole bouquet of roses." (5)

The Language of the Immaculate Heart

So these emanations of the Virgin's fragrance go back to a long tradition. A tradition which in the past expressed itself occasionally and locally, but tends today, it seems, to thrive.

"This language" in fact, is becoming here in Canada, more unbroken, nearly permanent. Many people have up till now experienced it, and in very different ways.

We are dealing here with a form of expression. Of a true language. And Our Lady uses this language in a subtle, multiform way, with a stunning versatility!

It is perceived in the presence of the statue, in the presence of the witness either with or without it. It manifests itself through objects which have touched the witness or the statue that weeps. Through the tears and without them. It adheres to objects which have touched the tears or the statue: prayer beads, medals, vigil oil, cloths, bags which carried the precious objects.

The fragrance is carried at distance with the objects that were embalmed with it.

It will also be perceived at a distance, without any intermediary. Many witnesses who have gone to pray to the Virgin in tears have benefited from this grace, to smell at a distance the fragrance of the Virgin. This experience has occurred at home, on the street, in the car, when taking a ride or going on errands. The Virgin manifests herself this way, either to attract the attention and solicit prayers, or to give an answer to a question, an exhortation, an encouragement or a consolation.

A visitor finds himself for the first time in front of Our Lady in tears. She welcomes him by exhaling her celestial fragrance. It is an exquisite invitation to bear witness.

A priest of the Marian Movement devotes much time by accompanying the Pilgrim Statue for many weeks. One night, he talks about the Marian message. To show him her contentment, the Virgin embalms his room with her fragrance of rose.

One person prays, and asks for a sign. She has lost the sense of smell. The Blessed Virgin allows her to perceive her fragrance. Double sign: an affirmative answer, and a temporal favor.

I do not want here to repeat what can be read in the numerous testimonials following the Third Part of this book. It mattered only to show how the language of the fragrance is both subtle, gracious and deliciously maternal.

(D) Mysterious Photos

From the first manifestations of the tears, the Virgin has asked Joseph Francis to put on film what he was witnessing. And these original photographs have right away taken on an unusual characteristic which has not contradicted itself afterwards:

THE BLESSED VIRGIN PROVIDES HERSELF THE SOURCE OF LIGHT NEEDED FOR THE SNAPSHOTS.

This lighting in fact comes either from the statue itself or from an enveloping source whose nature or origin no one can perceive. At the start the witness nevertheless used the natural light and an artificial light, comprising flashcubes. Later he will not be in need of any lithting. But the first photos are the combined results of the three sources.

At the time of the developing of the first film, the people in charge were perplexed. Moreover, certain photos have been taken in such conditions, that the results should have been, according to the laws of optics, more than disastrous. But the photos were a success.

Joseph Francis tells us that the Blessed Virgin presides over the take of the snapshots herself. She indicates to the seer how to place himself, how to hold the camera, what the angle of vision should be. Often, the mechanism will unlatch itself before he can press on the button.

All these photos which can be counted today in many hundreds, some of which illustrate this book, are another way for Our Lady to communicate with her children: those who for a question of distance or whatever other reason will not be able to come on the spot to honor her or pray to her.

A New Fact

Beginning in the summer of 1984, a new fact has occurred.

Up till then, the natural and the artificial lighting used inside with the flashcubes according to the needs, were combined to the "special effects" produced by the Blessed Virgin herself.

But, on August 24, 1984, the messenger was able to take perfect photographs without any light nearly. The photos reproduced in this book, starting with number (8) eight have been taken in the dark, or semi-darkness, with no flashcubes and this even in the middle of the night, under the sole faint and wan glow of a vigil lamp.

Photo number (8) eight was taken under such conditions. The light that we see at the bottom of the photo, to the left of the Madonna, is an illustration of the luminous source that Joseph Francis perceives and which will produce the lighting.

In the second photo, number (9) nine, the luminous source is in movement, like a whirlpool of light enveloping the statue. These photographic takes were willed, so it seems, to show that it is Our Lady who provides herself the lighting. All the photos after August 24, 1984, were taken in this fashion, under this mysterious lighting that I am at a loss to define.

The Woman Clothed with the Sun

Would it not be proper to recall here the description that is given to us of the "Virgin of Light" by certain well-known seers?

Melanie, shepherdess of La Salette, wrote:

"The Blessed Virgin was surrounded by two lights. The first light, closer to the Blessed Virgin, reached right to us; it shone brightly and scintillated. The second light went more around the Beautiful Lady, and we found ourselves within it. It was immobile, that is, it did not scintillate, but was much more brilliant than our poor sun of the earth. All these lights did not hurt or tire the eyes."

"Besides these lights, all this splendor, there came also groups or shafts of light or rays of light, from the Body of the Blessed Virgin, her clothes, from everywhere." (1)

In all these phenomena which surrounded or accompanied the apparitions of Fatima, was the light not in the foreground?

During the first manifestation of the Virgin, the children have first noticed a "flash". Then they found themselves *surrounded by a great light which practically blinded them...* In front of them, above the small tree, in the center of this great *aura of light* which envelops them also, they see a beautiful Lady, more brilliant than the sun. (2)

The other apparitions were also marked by the "light" emanating from the Virgin, or surrounding her as a divine aura. On the second visit, it appeared to the children that they were plunged "into a shaft of light". The one enveloping Jacinth and Francis was oriented towards heaven, the one around Lucy, turned towards the earth.

At Fatima, light therefore holds a great place, the solar phenomenon of October 13 being like the crowning, as this occured, besides, during other Marian manifestations.

The *Woman of the Apocalypse,* the Victorious One over the infernal Dragon does Saint John not describe her as *surrounded by light*?

"And a great sign appeared in heaven: A woman clothed with the *sun,* and the *moon* under her feet, and on her head a crown of twelve *stars*." (Apoc. 12, 1)

A Garment of Light

One day, a priest noticed that the garment of the pilgrim statue was brilliant, as if someone had applied some kind of polish to the statue. After verification, it was not that. The Virgin was expressing herself this way, to let her *presence* and her *joy* seen.

How not to compare with this fact the descriptions that Melanie of La

Salette gives us, as also Lucy of Fatima, of the "garment of light" of the Blessed Virgin? Melanie writes:

"The garment of the Blessed Virgin was white and silver and all brilliant; there was *nothing material*: it was *composed of light and glory*, changing and scintillating. On earth, there is no expression or comparison to give." (3)

More than twenty-five years after the apparition, Lucy comments thus on the way we should represent Our Lady of Fatima:

"It seems to me that if I knew how to paint - without being able to paint her as she really is, since it is impossible and that we cannot even describe her in words of the earth - I would only put a gown, as simple and as white as possible, with the "mantle" falling from the top of the head to the hem of the gown."

"And as I would not be able to paint the *light* and the beauty which adorned her, I would take away all the adornments except for a tiny golden thread on the edge of the mantle. This ornament shone on a *background of light* as if it had been a sunray shining more brilliantly than the rest. This comparison remains quite far from reality, but I do not know how to say it better." (4)

These details, which are more than mere details, let us glimpse the close concordance there is between Fatima and the manifestations whose sublime reality I am sketching here in broad lines. Let us not forget that the seer, Joseph Francis, has been trained by Our Lady, and that, from the time he has felt the need to do some apostolate, it is the Fatima message which has retained his attention and solicited his devotion.

There would be little efforts to make to show in depth the close relation which links to Fatima the Pilgrim Statue which rouses our interest here.

(E) She Passes Doing Good

What mission can accomplish the Blessed Virgin, Our Mother, if not a mission of salvation?

Let us precise. Our Lord, the Real and sole Redeemer has accomplished the whole of Redemption. He is the sole effective and complete cause for the Salvation of all humanity.

But humanity today has turned its back to salvation. The Christian nations themselves, forgetful of their origin, have pronounced the word of Lucifer: Non serviam! Rejecting the service of God, man pushes away in the same gesture the hand that alone can save him.

God, in his great Mercy, goes further on the road of salvation. He delegates the Mother of His Son.

What will then do Mary, if not recall to us, with her maternal love, the immeasurable Love of the Father and the Son for man.

And as Our Lord had passed doing good, by taking care of the body while healing the souls, Mary, the same way, will multiply the spiritual and temporal favors.

I shall not expose here to the reader a long list similar to that of Lourdes or of old sanctuaries which have seen multiply for centuries healings of all kinds and divine favors granted through the Mediatrix of all graces.

The Pilgrim Virgin that I now present here is relatively little known. A small number of faithfuls have had up till now the privilege to honor and invoke her maternal solicitude and obtain through her the favors requested.

But already Our Lady, through the Pilgrim Statue has spread many benedictions. This chapter does not pretend to be exhaustive, an impossible task for me, but only suggestive. May it though inspire those who have already benefited from particular graces or will be gratified with them in the future, to make them known to us, for the Glory of God and the Honor of Our Lady.

- A number of people had lost, completely or partially, the sense of smell. The emanations of the virginal fragrance of the Virgin have awakened the sense numbed by age or sickness.

- A person devoted to Our Lady and disfavored makes great efforts to follow the Pilgrim Virgin. He must travel long distances under unfavorable conditions. He suffers from a grave eye defect. One day he offers her flowers, and looks upon her with love. He is instantaneously cured.

- She was suffering from eye trouble. The medical treatments did not produce their effect as fast as she would have desired. An application of a piece of cotton-wool impregnated with the tears of the Virgin brought the desired relief. A complete and lasting cure.

- One person had suffered from a maternal indifference in her childhood. Having become a mother, her unsatiated need still weighed in her life. The tears and the maternal look of the Blessed Virgin are for her a grace of welcome and a cure which fills her heart with an unhoped-for maternal presence.

- One good Christian sees the statue animate itself: his apostolic sense is fortified by it. He will be a better apostle.

- Our families have lost the beautiful traditions which made them cells of prayer. The sight of Our Lady in tears, the exhalation of her fragrance have made of one of these families - and of many more - an apostolic home, a center of spiritual irradiation.

- One privileged soul of Our Lady generously engaged in the Marian apostolate, under the tearful eye of the Virgin sends to a friend a recording of hymns, testimonials, words of consolation, a recitation of the beads, and some photos of the Virgin in tears. It was a shock on the part of the one who receives this package. A life far from God makes place to conversion in tears of repentance. The new convert testifies of her happiness, and no doubt transmits in turn the grace of salvation received through the intercession of Our Lady and the beautiful collaboration of an apostolic soul.

- Many men and women have testified that their Christian life having undergone a subsidence, having ceased to practice, the Virgin in tears had operated in them a conversion and a new religious engagement.

Sorrows, anxieties, lack of affection, incomprehensions, disagreements: how many of these sorrows of the heart and the soul has the Virgin not cured by a single glance laden with love; by an emission of her fragrance of rose; by a single tear of compassion or a smile of consolation!

The Mother of Sorrows is also the Virgin of the Smile.

The Co-Redemptrix does she not identify herself with The One our beautiful litanies name the Mother of Salvation, the Gate of Heaven and the Queen of all the elect?

III

"WE ARE WITNESSES..."

In this third part are published without comments the personal testimonials of many people who have seen the statue, prayed in front of it, and through it benefited one way or the other from the favors and the maternal tenderness of Our Lady.

1 - To be Adopted by Mary...!

"About three years ago, while on a family outing, we stopped at our good friend Joseph Francis' place. We were seven: my husband and I, our four kids - three boys and a girl - and my elder brother."

"On entering his modest dwelling, we were caught unawares: a strong odor of rose embalmed the whole house. And to all evidence there were only artificial flowers at his place..."

"My little girl of four asked: 'Where are the roses...?'"

"Our friend led us to where throned a beautiful statue of Mary, the Mother of Jesus. Her presence in some way surrounded us, for in an instant we found ourselves kneeling at her feet, and interceding Her Son with Her."

"At that moment, we saw a small tear shine from her eyelid, slide slowly down her cheek and suspend itself from the chin. My brother got up, picked the little tear from the chin and traced the sign of the cross on my little girl's forehead and mine."

"My son of nine asked: 'Mother, why does she cry?'"

"Spontaneously I answered: 'Let us be silent in front of Mary for a few minutes, and maybe we shall know why.'"

"We prayed a while and suddenly, my youngest boy jumped and said, looking around: 'I know now, Mother! Mary loves us, and she needs our help to bring the world back to Her Son.'"

"'How do you know that?' I asked, kneeling."

"'Mary told me in my heart', and he darted away...'"

"That day I did receive a special grace. All during my growing days, I had felt a lack of affection from my mother. That day marked a great turning point in my life, through this statue. It was as if Mary had told me: 'I am your mother. My Son Jesus and I, we love you very much.'"

"And all the while I contemplated this magnificent statue, the image of our Heavenly Mother, tears streamed down my own cheeks, And She also cried!"

"What a joy to admire this statue of Mary, to hold it, to plunge an affectionate look into her eyes, and to think that the love, peace and joy she gives to me and others is only a glimpse of what the future holds."

"Later I had the privilege of receiving this beautiful statue in my home and to keep it for a while. How I was touched when my friends, the new and the old ones, came to visit her! She seems to be only a statue of the Virgin, but what a powerful instrument to attract souls to Her Son!"

"On certain occasions, I noted different expressions on her face, varying from a smile to tears. But always with this expression of goodness, tenderness and love."

"Many people told me they had received spiritual and temporal favors after having prayed in front of this statue. A young man who had just lost his mother confided to me that he had been consoled. Another person who was suffering from heart pressure received, after praying, a complete and instantaneous relief."

"Thank you, Mary, for your love! Thank you, Jesus, to share your love with us through the intermediary of your Mother!"

April 18, 1985   *Susan M. Miller*

2 - To the Little Ones, the Mysteries of the Kingdom

Young Colleen Miller, today 7 years of age, also had one day the privilege of visiting the "weeping Madonna", with her parents. She also received the attentions that Mary gives, through the intermediary of her image, to those who love her.

Could her testimony not touch us by its spontaneity, simplicity and candor?

"Her tears smell roses. I love her! She lets me think that I am special! I know she is really my Mother. She is so beautiful! Mary, thank you for giving me Your Son!"

April 18, 1985   *Colleen Miller, 7 years old*

3 - A Quarter of an Hour Filled with Eternity

"On November 17, 1982, while on a visit to some relatives, we learned that there was a weeping statue of the Virgin at Joseph Francis' place. Before returning home, we decide to pay him a visit, although we only had about fifteen minutes to spare. This quarter of an hour would change our lives."

"On arriving at his door, we heard some soft, tender music which did appear to come from within the house we were about to enter."

"We knock at the door. I felt as if deprived of my senses. Joseph Francis opens the door and lets us enter his humble dwelling. At the sight of the beautiful dear Mother of Fatima, I was so spellbound that I could not utter one word all the while our visit lasted."

"Before leaving, the proprietor of the statue gives us some oil from the vigil lamp of the Blessed Virgin, also some cotton-wool which has been dampened by the tears of the Virgin. Upon our return home, the Blessed Virgin will make us smell her fragrance: an odor of rose spread through the air. Afterwards, the same thing will occur on many occasions and in different places: at home, at church, and in the car when out for a drive. The children, as well as other people, have all noticed this odor."

"In attracting us to Her on that day, Our Lady of Fatima had a good reason. So she will tell her witness."

"What I can say, as the mother and with the other members of the family, is that our lives were completely changed on that day. Antoine, my husband, did not say his rosary; now, he recites it with us. We feel attached to Her as never before, and we pray to her a lot."

"Our piety is better than before. We cannot explain the things, but our hearts have been transformed, we feel more love for God and His Mother. It happens that we now pray during the night, as if Our Lady herself would wake us up to ask that we pray at that hour."

"We feel the need, more than before, to go to mass daily, go to communion, and do the way of the cross and other devotions like the first Saturdays of the month as asked by Our Lady of Fatima."

"We have understood that the Blessed Virgin had 'adopted' us and asked us to pray a lot. She also wants to show us her love and presence by offering the fragrance of her virtues."

April 1985

Irene Vienneau
Antoine Vienneau
Serge Vienneau

4 - How Mary Chooses Her Witnesses

"It was in the first week of 1983. I was then far from thinking that this would not be a year like the others for me, and there would happen some events both extraordinary and sorrowful."

"Everything began with a telephone conversation with my brother Antoine and his wife Irene, who live in the same village as we do. They had just arrived from a business trip. Our nephew they had visited had informed them about a statue of Our Lady of Fatima that had been weeping for approximately five years in that city."

"Very surprised, I ask the question: 'Is this all true?'"

"'But it is true', says Antoine, 'we dropped by to see her before coming back, and we have some photos.'"

"I cannot believe my ears. I do ask them all kinds of questions. A weeping statue, so close to us, and this for the past five years... These things always happen in other countries, yes, but here, in our country...!"

"It is nine o'clock at night, and my brother says: 'Come and see something nice.'"

"I did not wait to be begged."

"Indeed I am touched and attracted by the beauty and gentleness of her beautiful countenance, with tears on the cheeks and the chin. I cannot turn my eyes away from the sight, and I feel inclined to hold the Madonna tightly on my chest."

"'My sweet Jesus! Is this possible', I tell them. And they look at me and smile."

"But yes, why not? Why would our dear Mother of Heaven not show us her holy tears through this beautiful Madonna in Canada, as she does elsewhere on the planet? We do need it so much!'"

"They showed me afterwards pieces of cotton-wool which had received the tears and also a little bottle of oil coming from a vigil lamp kept nearby."

"They asked me to smell the good odor of rose which emanates from the cotton and of which they had the experience. Unfortunately, I cannot smell odors anymore. But they insisted that I put the cotton to my nose. I thought I did detect a delicate odor, but I am not sure."

"We talked for quite a while that night. Our hearts felt happy. Antoine and Irene told me in detail all about their short visit to the Madonna, and related their impressions. Never, they said, would they be able to forget her beautiful countenance."

"It is in the wee hours of the morning that they bring me home. I am not able to sleep the rest of the night. Pondering, I thought at once about certain people engaged in a Marian work who should be interested in these facts."

"In the meantime I contacted my nephew Frank in order to know more. On the telephone he told me that he knew well the proprietor of the statue, that it had been weeping for the past five years, that this mother and he had seen it in tears many times, etc."

"My nephew suggests that I call him myself and to come. He makes the offer to take me to his place. This would have pleased me; unfortunately, I had to take care of two sick persons, and I have some difficulty in speaking English, making it impossible to communicate easily with the seer who speaks English only."

"I ask my nephew to be my intermediary and send me some photos, a few pieces of cotton and some oil. He says he would gladly and as soon as possible."

"It did not delay. On January 13, I was happy to receive the package containing what I had asked for, with some spiritual leaflets and a letter from Joseph Francis."

"With the photos, the cotton and the oil in hands, I decided to talk all about it to my husband. I had kept silent up till then, because he was a man who liked to have proofs, and I waited to have something to show him."

"All of it keenly interested him. While I am telling him what I know, he keeps looking at the photos, touching them. He smells the cotton-wool and the oil, and remarks that '*he smells the odor of roses*'."

"I am surprised; as I know him, I expected him to say, 'It smells perfume', very simply. The fact being that in our family we are not familiar with the scent of roses. Thus I got the idea to make an experience with my children and grand-children."

"Jeannine is 35 years of age, Maurice, 29, Annette, 23, and the grand-

November 14, 1984
Stood the mournful mother sweeping...
(Stabat Mater)

28   November 14, 1984

"The Blessed Virgin cried nearly all the time
she talked to me."

(Mélanie, of La Salette)

29   November 14, 1984
"The tears of our tender Mother,
far from lessening her majestic air, of a Queen,
seemed to make her more beautiful..."
(Lucy, of Fatima)

30 November 26, 1984

"Above all, I am with you during these moments of darkness and suffering..."

(Message to Don Gobbi, 13/4/79)

31   November 26, 1984

My eyes shed streams of tears because
your law has not been kept.

(Ps. 119, 136)

32   December 1, 1984

"If only an enemy insulted me...
but you, my friend, my close friend?"

(Ps. 55, 13)

33   December 14, 1984
Oh, how sad and sore distressed Was the Mother...
Of the sole-begotten One!

(Stabat Mater)

34

December 14, 1984

If you do not listen to this in your pride,
I will weep in secret many tears...

(Jer. 13, 17)

children, Marco, 14, and Luc, 5. I make them smell the cotton-wool. Only Jeannine knew what it was, but all said: 'It smell roses', except for the youngest one, Luc, who said: 'It smells flowers...'"

"Afterwards, I chose among the photos the one which touched me the most. I place it in a protective transparent sheet and I hang it on the wall in order to look at it often. She is so beautiful! And I can thus join in the sorrows of the Blessed Virgin who makes them known to us by her Holy Tears through this beautiful statue."

"I then thought that the moment had come to pass this on to certain people who are apostles of the Blessed Virgin."

"I go through a great deception, For eight months, that is from January to September 1983, I take all kinds of steps to contact those who should have shown keen interest in the weeping Madonna. The arranged meetings are put off or cancelled. The priests and animators met are indifferent or occupied with something else. My efforts are left with just about no results."

"Faced with this small success, I asked myself: 'Is it I who do not know how to do things? It is true that I do not have the habit of insisting. Perhaps I should have...'"

An Attentive Soul

"I came to realize that it was the Blessed Virgin who chose her apostles and her witnesses. My deceptions would come to an end."

"One evening in September, Albert Arseneau arrives at my daughter Jeannine's where I was staying temporarily on account of sickness. He talked of his efforts to try and establish harmony between certain persons. We learn to know him better. He suffers and needs comfort. He no doubt found what he was seeking, for he comes again the next day."

"That day after he left, feeling that no doubt the Blessed Virgin sought to bring us closer, I decide to talk about the weeping Virgin, so I take a run home to get the photos. If the Blessed Virgin wants it, I shall show him the photos on his next visit."

"The 'next visit' was not long in coming: the next day, we are surprised to see his pickup truck appear in our driveway. It was not his habit to visit us that often. Especially on three consecutive days."

"The conversation which ensued gave me the occasion I was waiting for and the sign that I had to talk about the weeping Virgin. And right away he showed a great interest."

" 'Sid down', I said, 'I have something to show you.' "

"And I brought him the photos. He was visibly surprised."

" 'What beautiful photos! Look at the tears! She looks like the Virgin of Syracuse, but no, not altogether... Where did you get that? Since when have you got them?' "

"And I answered all his questions; he was so eager to know everything."

"For the rest of this narrative, Albert himself will say what he felt, and what he did."

"I had taken many steps, during long months, in order to interest other persons. And I had experienced many deceptions. And here, the latter, so near us, comes on his own, without our calling him and he pays attention, gets interested right away, as if he was putting himself a the Blessed Virgin's disposal, from the first word on our part."

"Having listened attentively to what I had to tell him, Albert could not get over it. He continued to look at the photos, moved and very happy from what he had just learned."

"And so was I! To see him happy, to see him get interested that way to the weeping Virgin... I had been waiting for so long for such a moment!"

"Albert then tells us: 'I now understand why I felt so drawn to come here these past few days!' "

May 22, 1985   *Marie De Gréchie*

5 - My Soul Glorifies the Lord!

"Was it a premonition?"

"In July 1976, during a pilgrimage in Italy, as I was passing in front of a painting of the Blessed Virgin hung on the wall behind the altar in a church in Milan, I saw something which from afar looked like a pearl drawn at the corner of one eye of the Madonna."

" 'That is funny', I said to myself. 'Is this the evocation of a past event translated this way?' "

"Observing more closely, I saw that it looked painted on, but sort of diffuse; perhaps was it not but a cluster of dust clinging on the painting and fixed by chance at the corner of the eye?"

"I did forget the incident until that Sunday of April 1985, when going in my mind over the events which I had lived for a year and half, this souvenir came back to my memory."

"So was this observation I had made, in Milan, a coincidence that occurred exactly one year before the first weeping which took place at Joseph Francis' on July 29, 1977?"

Photos That Talk

"It is at the home of Jeannine Aubé, daughter of Marie De Gréchie, and through the latter's intervention that I am put, for the first time, in the presence of photos representing the weeping statue."

"There comes from this statue such a profound feeling of sadness that is not easy to define. This is really unusual, and so close to us. So I do feel one should go and observe the fact on the spot. I thus consider the possibility of going to Joseph Francis'.

"But, how to introduce myself?"

"In the following days, this idea grows and incites me to write to present myself, at the same time giving my correspondent some information on a Marian Association to which I belonged."

"I expected an early reply, as I had made plans to go on the first weekend in October. The interval was short. The eve of my leaving arrives and no answer yet."

"I was still anxious to know whether or not the meeting could be arranged."

The Rendezvous

"I again make another attempt to reach the witness, through Marie and her nephew. Useless efforts. In the end, I am given Joseph Francis' telephone number with the suggestion that I perhaps should call, but I hesitate to contact him."

"Finally I decided, although it was not the proper time to reach him easily. It is 5 o'clock in the afternoon, and I had been advised to call him in the morning or later in the evening. I dialed just the same, taking a chance. And Joseph Francis answers!"

He confirms having really received my letter and that he is waiting for me. He gives me rendezvous for Sunday morning, October 2. 'It is the best time', he says, 'to receive you without being disturbed, and to have time enough to talk.'"

"He insists: 'I am waiting for you.'"

"Later I shall learn that he had already received a message regarding me, and that the Blessed Virgin had arranged things so we would get in contact for the benefit of her work."

"During the conversation, without knowing anything about the messages he had received, I was amazed and agreeably surprised to hear him talk as if we already knew each other. I was not unknown to him it seemed. Simple, affable, direct, free and easy, all surprising traits from someone that I had never seen before."

"I pass on the news to Marie De Gréchie who, in turn, is amazed by the way things are going. We exchange impressions, look at the photos, and then wait for the sequence of events. There remained to get ready, for a trip which, to me, was fair in distance."

"The next day, a Saturday, I board the train. But I do not feel as enchanted as before by this trip. At destination, I shall even feel a sort of repugnance. I do find myself quite naïve to run after what is perhaps just nonsense. I really feel flat. After finding hotel accommodations, I decide to go out to change my ideas. I go to the movies. On return, I feel my mind quite distant from my goal of the following day."

At Joseph Francis' Place

"It is Sunday, and I get up early to go to an 8 o'clock mass. It is rainy and dismal, and this is not to help the morale. The mass helps pick up my spirits. The celebrant is a bishop from the Philippines on a visiting tour of our country. I like his nice simplicity in the way to celebrate, as well as his homily, short but appropriate. He makes a delicate allusion to the troubles in his country, quite fitting with the reading of the day."

"I return to the hotel a little nonchalant, as if nothing extraordinary awaited me. I am in no rush. Yet, I was going to see the weeping Madonna!"

"I take in my hand the memo on which was inscribed the number to ring, and I dial. It is close to 9 o'clock."

"The communication is established. Joseph Francis inquires about my arrival, saying how sorry he is for not having received me as he would have liked. I understand that his modest dwelling makes it impossible for him to have the pleasure to accommodate visitors. In one hour he will be ready to receive me, to give him a call just before I leave."

"With this amiability, I regain my enthusiasm and my aplomb, but I remain intrigued by his fraternal air. Around 10 o'clock, I am on my way. The distance is not too far."

"It is in a wing attached to an old wooden house that Joseph Francis lives. In front of his door facing the street there is a small enclosure."

"I find myself in the presence of what appears to me as a smiling, but pale young man. I shall be amazed later on to learn that he is 39 years of age."

The Madonna with the Fragrance of Rose

"After the first words of greetings, I turn towards the beautiful statue of the Virgin of Fatima, about 40 in. high (1 meter approx.) that I had seen at the back of the room on coming in."

"But, what a beautiful statue! I am truly ravished by the unusual beauty of this statue. Never had I seen any like it, so beautiful. She has something particular, profound, live, natural."

"I thus express my feelings, and at the same time I feel intrigued by an odor of roses which seems to invade the room, at first subtly but then more and more strongly without becoming suffocating however. Still standing and looking, I mention this fact to Joseph Francis, telling him that I thought I had detected this odor on entering. I ask him if he had any roses in the room."

" 'No', he says. And he finds it amazing that so many people smell roses or a fragrance of some kind in his place, except him. He had not yet smelled these odors. Later he will detect them also."

The Beginning of a Friendship

"The conversation turns to other things, to continue non-stop. Noon arrives, then 1 o'clock, and we are still talking. At given moments, I make the move to go, and each time Joseph Francis appeared so happy to continue to conversation I did not dare to leave him. On one hand, I was afraid of imposing myself too long, and on the other, my presence seemed to please him greatly. He seemed glad to be able to talk, and I to hear him say so much! to learn so much! And the atmosphere was so fraternal, so relaxed; everything favored a prolonged conversation."

"We did not but talked. At one moment, I felt the need to kneel at the feet of the statue, with my host. A moment of silence. Then Joseph Francis started a prayer aloud, a prayer which was more like the expression of what he felt. He says why the Mother weeps: the approach of grave events, the corruption of the world, the situation in the Church, the abandonment by her children..."

"He falls silent, and we get up."

"During our lengthy conversation, he tells me that the Blessed Virgin had revealed to him that I would bring something which would please him, and this is confirmed when I give some information which aroused his interest greatly."

"He tells me also that after receipt of my letter he had prayed much and that the Blessed Virgin had told him to wait for me, to receive me like a brother, and not to worry about what to tell me. She recommended him to be simple and himself. And this was precisely the prayer that I had formulated to Our Lady on my part, to be as simple as possible, and not to say anything that could wreck plans."

"He told me things in confidence that I could not reveal but to certain chosen people."

A Warm Welcome by Our Lady

"During this first visit, the Blessed Virgin had thus the kindness of making me smell her fragrance of roses."

"Following this exceptional meeting, still 'dazed' by the accumulation of all what I had seen and heard, I put down in writing the results of this first experience."

"One week later, I gave a priest from Quebec City, some of the photos that I had on hand, with an envelope containing pieces of cotton-wool impregnated with the tears of Mary. A whiff of fragrance of rose arises to his nose to his great amazement."

"On my second visit to Joseph Francis, I came with another priest from Quebec, Father Jean-Paul Bélanger. The latter will narrate himself how his relation with the seer had been foreseen and arranged by Providence, and what were the signs given him by Our Lady to prove that she wanted to associate the two souls: a spiritual director and his protégé."

"I served as an intermediary to bring him Father Jean-Paul Bélanger, as other people I knew had played the same role between the seer and myself. Providence regularly utilizes our friendships, our human relations, to thus attract souls. We see in the Gospel, the future apostles naturally, so to speak, get introduced to one another, and one by another to the Master."

The Spiritual Director

"So, on October 24, 1983, I presented to my new friend the priest who would become shortly, following his acceptance, his Spiritual Director."

"Father Bélanger did not sleep much the night before. He takes advantage of this to pray the success of the important meeting of the next day. During this time, Joseph Francis is in dialogue with Heaven, receiving the visit of the Blessed Virgin who talked about what was in store for the following day. She gives him information regarding this event."

"It must be said that the Blessed Virgin had already announced to him that soon he would have a spiritual director, as he had often requested. He already knew his name before knowing who he was or from where. He had thought that 'Father Paul',as called by Our Lady, was a priest of his area, and he had even looked in the telephone book to try to locate him. Hence he was anxious to meet 'Father Paul'."

"Upon our arrival at Joseph Francis', the conversation started immediately between the two men. I stayed aside in order not to interfere in their conversation. Standing in front of the statue, Father Jean-Paul Bélanger also found it to be extraordinary in beauty and expression."

"Some information regarding a Marian movement is given, as well as the request of the Blessed Virgin that he became the spiritual director of Joseph Francis. The request is accepted."

The Tears of Mary

"And I saw this beautiful statue cry... at different times. A first time during my second visit at Joseph Francis', in the fall of 1983. Each time the tears were abundant.They could be seen flowing from the eyes of the statue as when we see a person cry. And her expression is so sorrowful! It is really Our Lady in person who grieves! The tears flow, stream down the cheeks, and hang on the chin before falling. During the second weeping I witnessed, I wiped the tears with a scapular, which later had the scent of roses. I dared taste these tears; they were lukewarm..."

Another Weeping

"It is in November 1983, on my third visit to this privileged soul of Our Lady. Before even crossing the doorway, I was met by a strong odor of roses. How not to be amazed to smell roses outside, on a windy, rainy and rather wintry weather of November"

"After a few words of greetings, I help Joseph Francis take off a transparent plastic sheet covering the statue to protect it: some soot leaks out from a dilapidated oil-stove used to heat the dwelling."

"It is then that I notice the tears. Occupied in putting away the protective sheet, my host has not seen anything yet. At my call, he looks up and kneels down."

"According to the message he then receives, the Virgin is crying out of joy, and my companion must immediately take 'three photos', she tells him. He then tells me that it is not he who 'directs things'; it is the Blessed Virgin herself who indicates the angle to shoot, and often 'presses' on the button of the camera."

"On December 18, 1983, I am again on visit. Around 11 o'clock in the morning, I step out to go and get some photos Joseph Francis had developed. On my return, I find him in a stir: the Virgin of Fatima has started weeping during my absence. Indeed, she is shedding tears."

"It is disquieting. Soon it is over, but there still remains big tears hanging from the chin. I thought I had noticed, on leaving, what appeared to be the beginning of a weeping, but thinking I was wrong, I had said nothing."

"We then look at the photos I had brought back: what a surprise to see in such beautiful colors, so clear, the statue of Our Lady of Fatima in tears!"

The Fragrance of Roses

"On many occasions I smelled the scent of roses. I first smelled it on my first visit, as I said above. Then a month later, when I was back in November. It was a real end-of-the-fall day: gusts of wind and freezing rain, nothing to suggest such a fragrance. And it is outside, as I was approaching the house where the seer lives, that I smelled this odor, after getting out of a taxi. The first time, on the contrary, I was inside."

"Later, also in November, in the train that was taking us to Quebec, Joseph Francis, me and some other friends, I again perceived the same phenomenon. He had taken the train in his hometown, and I joined him later in the day. At the station, he was at one end of the sleeping car, but I went in at the other end. On entering the bedroom I was sure I was in the right place as the odor was floating in the air. He had placed a small statuette on the window sill of the car. This odor remained all the time we busied ourselves looking at the magnificent photos he was bringing with him."

"This fragrance also transmits itself through different objects or substances which have been in contact either with the statue or the seer. Such as the samples of oil from the vigil lamp that Joseph Francis gives to certain persons. He had given me a bottle in October 1983, at the time I first met him, and the odor from this oil lasted over a year."

"One day, I forgot my prayer beads at his place, a souvenir from my deceased father. Joseph Francis placed the case at the feet of the weeping Madonna. Some tears fell on it. I got it back latter; it was embalmed with the scent of roses. I left it in the open on my dresser, and to this day, May 8, 1985, at the time of writing these lines, a light odor still persists."

"This phenomenon can also manifest itself for other reasons and in some other way. The Blessed Virgin often projects her fragrance at a distance - but is she not then present? - to give, we could say, a message. One day, I had the definite feeling of a presence around me. My mother had just talked to me about an Italian priest who apparently has the stigmata. For some time I had a question in my mind concerning him. At the moment we talked about this priest, I clearly felt a presence around me. I communicated with Joseph Francis and the latter assured me that I had just had the visit of our heavenly Mother."

"My traveling bag seems to have acquired the capacity to retain this odor of roses. I take it regularly to Joseph Francis'. Afterwards the objects placed in this bag emit a fragrance of roses or field flowers."

"I could add many other cases of the kind."

"It does seem that the Blessed Virgin uses her fragrance to rejoice her children and manifest to them her presence and maternal sentiments."

"Hence I learned one day by telephone that Joseph Francis had been questioned by Our Lord on this, following my visit to his place on November 12."

" 'How did your 'big brother' (Albert) like the reception my Mother gave him: fragrance of rose before coming in, and tears of joy during his visit?' "

A Spiritual Friendship

"Being now bonded to Joseph Francis since our first meeting, by a friendship taking its source in the Immaculate Heart of Mary, and which makes the two of us brothers in Christ, I realize the grace of great value this fact represents of being able to participate so to speak in the privileges which are now part of his daily life."

"I am always amazed when I hear Joseph Francis calmly state that he has seen a celestial being or received a message. He talks about it as a natural thing, as if everyone in the world could have this kind of experience."

"All of this has become familiar to him, but his narratives always keep a reserve, a profound mark of respect, and his eyes brighten as he narrates... He keeps the candor of a child in his expressions and sentiments. As well as a warmth full of reverence..."

"Is it because of his candor, his simplicity, his overture to the supernatural and his humility that the Blessed Virgin has chosen to reveal to him, primarily to him, and through him to us, the sight of her sorrow and her need for compassion and prayers?"

May 8, 1985   *Albert Arseneau*

6 - ...So I Can Testify!

"Sunday, August 19, 1984, I brought the statue back from Quebec City in order to hand it over to its proprietor, Joseph Francis. We had given ourselves rendezvous at a motel where reservations had been made for us through the care of Albert Arseneau, the loyal guardian of the seer. We were to stay two days, that is from Sunday to Tuesday. But in fact our stay was prolonged one more day."

"Joseph Francis arrived towards the end of the day. Our two respective rooms were adjoining. I had put down the statue in my room where it stayed until the following day."

"I make a note here on an important point in the life of the seer: each afternoon, he prays for about two hours. This meditation is often accompanied by sufferings; messages are communicated to him and often, the Virgin lets her tears fall."

"That night, she visited him, accompanied by Saint Bernard, and certain things were imparted."

"The Blessed Virgin revealed with sadness the reason why of certain difficulties within the Church and within a Marian Association. She complained of the unfaithfulness of certain people. These complaints were intermingled with teachings of a mystical order and secrets which it is not opportune to divulge here. Exhortations are added to informations. For example, we should be reading more of the lives of Saints, those of Canada, and the mystics. We would gain to know them better in order to imitate them."

"The saints had to suffer much, as for example Saint Louis Grignion de Montfort. The wound which made Our Lord suffer the most was the wound of his shoulder."

"Is it not better to ponder over these counsels addressed to us for our spiritual advancement rather than halt on things we cannot change?"

Monday, August 20, 1984

"After dinner, as was agreed upon, I brought the statue over to Joseph Francis' room and I placed it on the small dresser in the room."

"Later he sees a light surrounding the statue."

"He enters his period of meditation, mentioned above. Messages were given. The Blessed Virgin asked the three of us to remain one day extra at that place. But she did not insist. Her 'request' was delicate and appealed to our good will. 'If they care', she says, meaning if they want to. 'It would please me', she adds. The invitation is accepted by the three. Albert would come to join us in the afternoon at the time he could."

"We can admire the gentleness of the Mother of God. She does not impose, she suggests, she appeals to our good will, even though the hour is crucial and things to do are important."

"She let fall complaints from her lips. Then the tears flowed. Joseph Francis, saddened, asks: 'Is it because of me you are crying?'"

"New complaints accompanied by tears give the witness to understand that he is not the cause. He is the confidant saddened by the sighs of the Mother of Sorrows, unable to reach the heart of her rebel children."

"No doubt to console Herself, the Virgin looks at him and thinks about those who are with him. She says: 'Your director and Albert have been very generous towards you. They now suffer much. Your director needs rest. I shall fill his heart with spiritual strength for the future.'"

"'Even though you want to come 'Home', we still need you here. You have to pray and save many souls."

"This series of messages was accompanied by a prolonged intermittent weeping, with moments of greater intensity. It lasted in all for about two hours."

"As many words and different sentiments are expressed by the Blessed Virgin, her tears sometimes take a different import."

"Thus she tells Joseph Francis, for instance: 'I am also crying with joy, to see you together.'"

"And saying that, she smiles."

"Around 4 o'clock, Albert arrives at his friend's. Seeing the Virgin in tears, he calls me. I immediately go in to catch the last of the weeping."

"It was the first time I was seeing the statue shed tears."

"Indeed I could see tears running down the cheeks, down the body of the statue and fall on the furniture. Already there was on that piece of furniture, in small spots, traces of dried tears. Once fallen, the tears rapidly evaporate, leaving on certain surfaces a ring which is not erased easily. This is what I then observed."

"Afterwards, Joseph Francis told us, according to the memory he had of it or the one which the Lord left him, the messages that he had received during the two preceding hours."

"It is not always opportune to communicate publicly the tenor of what he receives.Each one has its own reason. Certain information is meant for the subject himself, for his sanctification or for the future of the Church. All will be told in due time, according to the necessity or the opportunity. And, curiously, the messenger often forgets what has been told to him until the moment he has to reveal it. I was a witness to this kind of happening."

"The Blessed Virgin told Joseph Francis, that day, that she had become a pilgrim on the day of the Incarnation, and that she would hold that role until the end of the world."

Tuesday, August 21, 1984

"It is 9 a.m. I find myself with Joseph Francis. He then reports what he has seen and heard during the preceding night. The Blessed Virgin thanks us for having accepted to stay an extra day."

" 'Because of that',she says, 'we shall give you special graces, to you and to Rolande also.' "

"Mrs. Picard was in fact to be with us in thought for the nocturnal prayer asked by Our Lady. A special exhortation meant for Albert is communicated to him."

"That night, Joseph Francis received the undesirable visit of the Wicked One, a thing which repeats itself from time to time. His guardian angel came to his help. Wearisome combats always take place during these moments. He accepts the great sufferings offered to him. Our Lord has asked him to bear with him his crowning of thorns. I was able to notice the wounds possibly made by three thorns embedded in his head. These wounds heal in a few hours."

"Among the messages received, we can note these:

- The Blessed Virgin asks many prayers for the priests.

- She complains that they do not pray nor fast as they should in the communities.

- If we do not change, certain calamities and social upheavals will occur."

"Then she announced: 'I shall be back this afternoon.' "

The Afternoon

"After the noon meal, I carried the Madonna over to Joseph Francis' room for his period of prayers in the afternoon."

"Around 4 p.m. Albert arrives from his home."

"He decides not to go in immediately but to call him through the window. Was he asleep or plunged in profound meditations? In any case he came to at the calls of his companion."

"In turn I arrive and go in. The room was in obscurity, the only light at the time of our arrival coming from the open door. I then notice, in the light coming from outside, the statue in tears. Neither of my two companions having noticed anything yet it seems."

"I can then see the eyes affected by a sort of swelling which bursts and lets out a flow of tears which runs down the cheeks to join under the chin and fall on the piece of furniture."

"Without hesitation I call out to Joseph Francis: 'The statue is weeping!'"

"And at the same time I extend my hand to gather with my finger these effusions from the eyes of the statue and to bring to my lips. To the taste it does feel like human tears... And I think about the pictures that should be taken to testify to this: 'Joseph Francis, do you have your camera?'"

"'Yes', he answers, 'but I do not have any flash.' And the idea comes to take the statue outside to take advantage of the natural light of the day to take the photos. A complete film of twelve poses is used. And at the take of the snapshots, the important part of the weeping is over. The flow had gushed inside and during the short distance of carrying it outside. But the photos are just the same quite revealing. They will show a kind of aura surrounding the whole statue.!"

"I had just been given visually the irrefutable proof, contrary to the pretensions of those who have seen but trickery, that there could not be absolutely anything of the kind."

*** *** ***

"This weeping constituted for me a double attestation."

"I shall first say that on the testimoy of trustworthy people, I already believed without having seen myself the statue shed tears. I was adhering too because of the other signs which accompanied the event, signs relevant to the message itself: what I had seen of Joseph Francis' life, his behavior, the messages he transmitted, the events in which they were circumstanced and those I had myself lived for nearly a year now. All that was consistent and constituted, as far as my judgement was concerned, a presumption of authenticity."

"Nevertheless, without doubting in anything whatsoever, I felt a problem arise for me. On the eve of that day, I had asked myself: 'In front of the unbelievers what could I do? It is impossible to testify for myself that the Virgin is weeping: I have not seen her shed tears myself.'"

"I was not requesting anything in thinking that, I was only stating my inability to testify according to my own experience. I did not in any way force the hand of the Blessed Virgin: we do not have orders to give her. That was my conviction, and the answer I gave, one day, to someone who was advising me as the spiritual director of the seer, to command the Virgin to show me her tears. 'We do not give orders to the Blessed Virgin', I had answered."

"This weeping was an answer to my question. The Blessed Virgin made good the lack I felt by giving me her own sign: her tears, and abundantly: 'I had seen her cry!'"

"Always so good - may She be blessed - the Blessed Virgin added to that sign by communicating through her messenger the reason of the tears. This information became for me another sign."

"Joseph Francis did not know what had preoccupied my mind the day before, what I exposed above. Now the very night of this blessed day, I received the following communication which he gave me the next morning: 'It is for your director that I cried, so he can testify for himself.'"

"I add on my behalf: 'So I can confirm that in all of that there is no human intervention.!'"

*** *** ***

"It is suggested that I give an account of my impressions at the time these events took place. How to describe what we can feel in front of such a phenomenon? Facts are noticed and we report them. The impressions are lived inside. It is sometimes appropriate to make them known; sometimes it is better to keep them in the heart."

"Regarding the why and wherefore of the tears or the mystic phenomena, only the Lord, the Blessed Virgin or the saints involved have the right or the power to judge their pertinence or to make them known."

"It is not new that the Blessed Virgin speaks and weeps. She does it more today more frequently and more intensely. Has the world taken notice up till now? We cannot give more explanation that the fact itself: 'The Blessed Virgin speaks and weeps to strengthen her pressing call to conversion and a return to God.'"

"Is it her LAST CALL?"

March 25, 1985   *Father Jean-Paul Bélanger*

7 - Our Lady's Fragrance Accompanies Us

"It is on October 7, 1983, on the train taking us to Cap-de-la-Madeleine, in Quebec, that we have seen the first photo of the weeping Madonna of Joseph Francis. Albert Arseneau, who showed us the photos he carried with him, had also in his hands some cotton-wool impregnated with the tears. A scent of rose was exuding from it. This communication was made discreetly considering the presence of other passengers."

"Later, in November, on the first trip that Joseph Francis was making to Quebec City with Albert, we had the opportunity to meet him. Not being in the same car, as we were traveling at night, Albert introduced us to Joseph Francis, at the station in Lévis."

"Joseph Francis had with him five small sealed glass-containers, in the shape of a tear, each containing a rose floating in water. Each of the five containers had a rose of different color, and four ot them were destined to four identified persons. But as for the fifth one, Joseph Francis did not know who it was meant for before meeting us. On meeting us he receives the message that it was meant for Béatrice."

"Some weeks, following our return home, Albert comes to say the rosary with our prayer group. He had on him a souvenir from his departed father, a rosary which smelled roses. These beads had been placed around the hands of the weeping statue, on a visit he had made to Joseph Francis' place, at a time when the Pilgrim statue had wept."

"The cotton-wool soaked with the tears and the oil from the vigil lamp that we received from Joseph Francis also had the fragrance of rose."

"Later we received a photo of the weeping Virgin taken by Joseph Francis in complete darkness, and at a time he had no flash in his camera."

April 1985   *Béatrice Haché*
                                                          Alban Haché

8 - She Recovers Her Sense of Smell

"Friday, October 26, 1984, I was invited by some friends to a meeting of information of the Marian Movement and to recite the rosary."

"On arrival, Susan Miller greeted me saying that Joseph Francis was here with the statue of Our Lady of Fatima, and that the statue was weeping. Entering the living room, I saw it... The eyes were visibly wet as were the cheeks, and a tear hung from the chin."

"A fragrance of rose was very pronounced in the room and our hostess said that the scent came from the tears of Our Lady. Later on in the evening, I am given a piece of the cotton-wool which had absorbed the tears. A strong fragrance or rose exuded from it, and still continues to this day, although more faintly."

"I must mention here that a woman who had lost the sense of smell perceived the fragrance of rose after having asked the Virgin to give her a sign that one of her prayers had been heard."

"I really do not know how to describe my feelings at this stage. I had heard talk about the statue before, but without paying too much attention. I had nearly forgotten. I felt very unworthy of the privilege of seeing the tears of Our Lady, and I asked myself why God was giving me the favor of being present at that meeting, with such good people. I offended God so much in my life that I acknowledge being unworthy of such a favor. I consecrated myself and my children to the Immaculate Heart of Mary, and since that date, I am trying more than ever before in my life, to know and do the will of Mary and that of God."

*** *** ***

"Friday, November 2, I was again invited by my friends, Jim and Susan Miller, to come and join them for the recitation of the rosary. They asked me to pick Joseph Francis and a friend who lived on the way. On arriving at Joseph Francis' place, we noticed that the statue was in tears. We were surprised. Having seen the statue weep the preceding Friday, this was a new surprise."

"Hesitating, I asked Joseph Francis if I could make the sign of the cross with a tear hanging from the chin of the Madonna."

"He consented. Mrs J. Richard asks and obtains the same privilege... After staying an hour at his place, we went to see those who had invited us."

35   December 1984
"My time has now come: this extraordinary intervention
of mine must be clearly recognized by all."
                    (Message to Don Gobbi, 23/6/79)

36   February 2, 1985
Virgins of all virgins best, let me share thy grief.
(Stabat Mater)

37 February 2, 1985

"… I say it again today with my tears."

(Phis. 3, 18)

38   January 22, 1985
"O Mary! My Mother! Is it for me that you cry so?"
                                        (A witness)

39   January 22, 1985

Through her heart... All His bitter anguish bearing...
                                        (Stabat Mater)

January 22, 1985

My eyes torment my soul.

(Lam. 3, 51)

41   January 24, 1985
I am overwhelmed with grief.
                                         (Tob. 3, 6)

42

January 24, 1985

"My good mother, do not cry! I want to love you for
all humanity on earth."

(Mélanie, of La Salette)

"Naturally Joseph Francis came with us with the statue. We were indeed happy of the fragrance of rose which could be scented during the whole evening. It came at intervals, sometimes strongly, at other times more moderately, but it lasted the whole evening."

"I must mention that the woman, who had lost her sense of smell and had recovered it the preceding week, could also smell the fragrance at the same time we did, and in the same way as those with a normal sense of smell."

*** *** ***

"I cannot describe everything that I have seen or felt through this privilege. Joseph Francis always repeats to us that all that is the work of God and Our Lady..."

November 6, 1984   *L.M.*

9 - Tears That Cure

"In the month of January, 1983, my mother telephones me to tell me that she had received through my cousin Frank Vienneau some beautiful photos of a statue of the Virgin of Fatima that has been weeping for the past five years at someone's home. She had also received some wads of cotton which had absorbed the tears, and a small bottle of oil which came from the vigil lamp placed near the apparently miraculous statue."

"I am therefore quite eager the next morning to go to my mother's place to see the photos. It was so moving to look at them, and I noticed the fragrance of rose coming from the pieces of cotton-wool and the little bottle of oil. My mother says that she cannot smell anything. She then gives me as a gift a little piece of the cotton-wool and also some oil that I preciously take home with me."

"Later, in December of 1983, I had a problem: one morning I feel tears running continuously from my left eye. Thinking that it would diminish, I do not worry. But the days go by, and the weeks, and still it continues. It is only at the end of January that I made up my mind to see a doctor, for I must say that I am 'allergic' to doctors and hospitals."

"On seeing my eye, the doctor immediately sends me to a specialist who noticed that the tear duct is obstructed. He prescribed some drops to be put everyday for two months. If that does not succeed, he adds, it will be the hospital, and we will have to clear the passage ourselves."

"The medicine does not produce results, and my eye continues to run more than ever. Fearing the hospital, I do not return to see the specialist right away. As there were still a few drops left for two weeks, I continued the treatment hoping."

"Some days later, during the night of Holy Saturday, my eye began to hurt. I hardly slept. When I got up the next morning, Easter Day, my eye was red and swollen."

"I told myself: 'I delayed too long! I must resign myself to go to the hospital.' My mother who was with me, says: 'Indeed your eye does not look well.' "

"It is then that I notice that my eye has stopped running. We did not know what to make of it: 'Is it worse, or is it better?' "

"After a few days, the redness left completely and my eye returned to normal."

"This happened on April 22, 1984. Since that day, I do not have any more problem with my eye."

"We owe much thanks and gratitude to the Virgin of Fatima who has cured my eye with her blessed tears!"

May 20, 1985   *Jeannine Aubé*

10 - What a Beautiful Anniversary Gift!

"It is on the occasion of a religious ceremony, in November of 1983, that I met Joseph Francis. He was then on a visit in Quebec, accompanied by Albert Arseneau and Father Jean-Paul Bélanger to attend a Marian celebration."

"Afterwards he would come to my house with the two same people. On one of these visits, a celestial atmosphere pervaded us, and I understood that my visitor brought with him a particular grace from the Blessed Virgin, which in the occurence inundated my home with a celestial joy."

"On another trip later, he had with him his Pilgrim Virgin, but he could not leave her in my home despite the desire I then had to receive her. Nevertheless I was able, for a few minutes, to contemplate her so beautiful countenance! And I attended, that day, a ceremony during which she was enthroned, and this permitted me to appreciate her presence and inexpressible beauty better."

80

"It is during the summer of 1984, in July, that I had the joy of receiving her home. Having sustained an insult some week before, she came to my home with an expression of sadness one could not define. To me, to receive her in my house on the day of my birthday was a favor of great worth from Heaven. It came about that she stayed in my home for nearly a month."

"At the beginning of her stay, everyone remarked how sad she seemed. But little by little, the sadness gave way to joy. Indeed it is remarkable to see how this statue has a live expression, reflecting different moods of the soul. I think that she wants to express this way the sentiments she has, either for us, for sinners, or for the sad situation in the world and the Church, etc. And we feel drawn into sharing her emotions and to pray her with more fervor in order to console her."

"It is on the very day of her arrival that she let me see her tears. Therefore, I can also testify that the Pilgrim Virgin of Joseph Francis really weeps. I SAW HER, in my home, shed a few tears, and I was alone praying. I shall add that I had not asked this miracle, as I already believed."

"It was in the evening. I was saying my rosary, while contemplating her. Then I saw appear a few tears, but curiously enough this did not make me sad. The tears lasted but a few minutes, and I got the impression that the Virgin was telling me her 'joy' to have been welcomed with love, while others had reject her. And her tears left me with the 'shared' joy, by me on one hand to have this so beautiful and good Madonna, by the Blessed Virgin on the other to feel welcomed and loved."

"Later in a message, through Joseph Francis, it was confirmed that my impressions had been right, these tears had really been tears of joy."

"As the days went by, the sadness expressed on her countenance diminished and at the end was gone. Everybody could notice the live expression of the Pilgrim Virgin. She seemed to follow our movements as we walked in her presence. I often felt that her gaze scrutinized me, but this impression did not cause me any worry, on the contrary."

"How not to love so good a Mother!"

"And how not to welcome with joy and gratitude her calls to conversion, for the gift of self for a fruitful apostolate!"

March 25, 1985   *Rolande Picard*

11 - A Month with the Pilgrim Virgin

"Here is my personal experience concerning a pilgrim statue of Our Lady of Fatima."

"On February 10, 1985, I arrived by plane in Charlottetown, where I met Father Paul Egan, pastor of St. Theresa Parish, in Morell, Prince Edward Island. On his part, traveling by car, David McCormick came to join us, bringing with him a magnificent statue of Our Lady of Fatima. For our visits across Prince Edward Island, accompanying this pilgrim statue, we resided for more than a week at Father Egan's presbytery."

Beauty and Fragrance

"The first thing I observed with this statue I had never seen was its great beauty. And then I noticed the scent of rose which came from it as I would get close. I smelled this perfume throughout the whole month I accompanied the pilgrim statue. It was noticeable in a varied way: sometimes lightly, at other times intensely."

"Many remarkable things happened during these weeks of traveling. The first to come about happened in Father Egan's office. He more or less believed in these phenomena that many people talked about. He presumed that people were all disposed to invent such things. After two days of presence of the statue in the presbytery, on entering his office, he was greeted by a strong scent of rose. He called Lucille the housekeeper to ask her if she had sprayed some air purifier in the room. She answered no, but that she also had smelled this strong odor. The statue embalmed this part of the house for nearly a whole day. Father Egan will later admit that the event had convinced him the emanation did come from the statue of the Blessed Virgin, and will yield under the evidence."

The Tears

"During our visits across the island, among the faithfuls who came to see the statue and pray at her feet, many affirm to have seen tears flow from the eyes. Others perceived the scent of rose. Two reported having seen tears flow during mass. So this I could not affirm."

His Sight Is Corrected

"A young man of 35 from Charlottetown hitch-hicked in order to come to the places where we stopped with the statue. In Vernon River, he brought a white rose which he laid at her feet. And then went to sit in the first pew in front of the statue."

"Jos. Arseneau, his name, suffered from a severe eye defect: he had double vision. After an operation to the eyes which was a total failure, his two eyes functioned with no convergence, each image being distinct from the other, so much so he always saw double objects. Also, things appeared to him deformed. He was therefore seeing a double statue. But as he was looking at it, the double vision became one. He saw but one statue. His vision was corrected."

"I had the occasion of seeing Jos. Arseneau again. One night, on the way from Vernon River to Morell, we noticed a young man signaling for a place in our car. We recognized him as he climbed in. He told us that the moment he went to his place at the feet of the Madonna, the double vision he had of Her fused into one, and for the first time saw but one object. His vision is now normal."

"He stayed with us that night to leave in the morning for Charlottetown. I asked him to see his doctor again, an eye specialist, in order to verify if his normal vision would remain, and I asked him to write to me when he would have the results of the test."

A Garment of Variable Color

"Later, I followed the Pilgrim Virgin to Brook Village, Nova Scotia, to St. John the Baptist Parish. Father Dennis Campbell who was receiving the Madonna in his parish had invited a few people to come before the evening mass."

"We were about five or six, assembled around the statue. Father Campbell suddenly noticed that the garment of the statue which was white up till then started to become blue. He drew our attention to this. And looking in turn, we saw that it had for the good part become blue, while a part was still white. But soon this part also turned to the same blue."

"I stayed at the presbytery and so did Father McLeod. One day, as I was in prayer in front of the statue which was with us, I thought I noticed that the garment was rose colored. Continuing my prayer, the garment in front of my eyes turned yellow. This surprised me very much, as yellow is one of my favorite colors. Thinking to be victim of my imagination, I went closer to the statue to see better, and I persisted in looking to assure myself that it was really yellow. The gown was in fact yellow. The next day, when I returned to see the statue, the pleats and the gown had returned to a light rose."

In Truro: a Fragrance of Rose

"In Truro, in the Immaculate Conception Parish, I preached on an important Marian movement. The statue had been placed in the church. When I returned to my room, I noticed a strong scent of rose. As there was in the adjoining bathroom a perfumed soap recently unwrapped, I thought that the odor could come from the bar of soap. I went out and later came back to my room, to notice again this strong scent of rose. It still seemed that this came from the soap. The next morning after having stepped out, I returned to my room. The bar of soap was still there but the odor had vanished. This convinced me of the veracity of the testimonials which had come to my ears. I had remained sceptic up till then regarding the perfume. Being a psychologist, I believed that people made their own "projection" on the statue. Following this event, I came to the evidence that the statue really emitted on different occasions a fragrance of rose."

"This scent often reveals itself and in variable fashion. Sometimes strong, it can also be light. Many instances of the kind occurred during my trip."

The Hue of the Face

"One day, I was to celebrate mass in a church in New Brunswick. Passing in front of the statue on my way to the altar, I noticed that the hue of the Virgin had become pale. I thought it was a light effect. After mass, I examined the thing more closely. Her countenance in fact was very pale."

"Going over all that in my mind, I am brought back to the messages or interior locutions that had received Father Stefano Gobbi, of Milan, messages which have been published and distributed throughout the world by his spiritual director, Father Renzo."

"One of the messages in particular concerns everything which precedes. It is the message of January 24, 1984. We can read the following:

'A sign also of how much I like the fitting veneration given to my images is what I am effecting through this little statue. It is a triple sign I give you: that of my eyes, which suddenly come alive; that of the color of my countenance, which changes its hue; and that of my Heart, which exudes a fragrance, now a delicate one, now one of greater strenght.' (...)"

It is the whole message that could be cited. [1]

" 'By the sign I give you in the color of my visage, I want to show you that I am a Mother for all, and today I share in all your joys. But I also suffer in all your numerous sufferings.'

---

[1] See Appendix 2.

'When a mother is happy and jumps for joy, you see the color of her face become rosy; when she is worried about the fate of her children you see her face turn completely pale.'

'If this happens to an earthly mother, it also happens to Me, and the sign I give you, so human and maternal, is to tell you that as a Mother I truly share in all the moments of your mortal life.' "

"It is only after having noticed the paleness of the face of the statue that I became aware of this message. Up till then, I still doubted my own vision, but after reading what is preceding I understood and was convinced."

From the Maritimes to Ontario

"And so, the pilgrim statue traveled a whole month with David McCormick and myself throughout the Maritimes. Many people at its sight were profoundly touched. I am only giving here the story of things of which I was a direct witness. In reality many other things occurred in relation to the weepings. I prefer to leave it to others the care of recounting them."

"Shortly after this trip in the East, David McCormick, the carrier of the statue, undertook another tour with the pilgrim statue in Ontario."

"She made a halt in our chapel. Fifteen priests live at the residence. Many are, naturally, sceptics regarding such phenomena."

"But one day, a confrere, assistant-superior and teacher at our institution, came to me and said: 'I have become a convert!' "

" 'What do you mean?' I asked."

" 'I have become converted', he repeats. 'I was praying in front of the statue of the Blessed Virgin. Her cape, naturally, is white. During my prayer it went from white to blue. I must admit that there is something miraculous in that statue.' "

"Such events repeated themselves. Hence one day, while in a presbytery, I was looking at the statue which was sojourning. A few minutes before the housekeeper had made her routine round with the furniture polish. Having sat down in the room after she had passed I noticed that the cape had become very brilliant. I made the remark to David who had been in the room at the time of the housekeeper's visit."

" 'I see that the housekeeper has not forgotten the statue with her furniture polish.' "

" 'Not at all', he answers, 'I was here and I can assure you that she did not touch the statue.' "

Conclusion

"These happenings concerning the color of the cape of the Madonna repeated themselves, as I have said. During my visit at Father Campbell's presbytery, in Brook Village, in Nova Scotia, the cape had become blue and I recalled afterwards that it was white before."

"These events, like many others regarding the statue, contribute to make us aware of the presence of God, namely Jesus, the Holy Ghost, the Holy Trinity."

"These occurrences came about during a certain period of time. I had not jotted down anything; it is only later that the idea came to consign them in writing. In gathering all these facts, I cannot but yield to the evidence: it is my personal conviction that this statue is really the authentic sign of the presence of the Blessed Virgin on earth, according to the messages She Herself gave to Father Gobbi:

'As a mother I wish to speak to you, I who am here with you, represented by the statue you have here. Every statue of mine is a sign of my presence, and reminds you of your heavenly Mother. Therefore each of them should be honored and put in a place of greater veneration.'"

April 5, 1985   *Father X*

12 - I Saw the All Beautiful Weep

"This is Tuesday, January 30, 1985, I am on a trip with my son Marc. We take advantage of our stay to visit Joseph Francis."

"We arrive at his place around 1:45 p.m. As we go in, our attention is immediately drawn to a fragrance of rose which embalms the house. The Virgin is there, right besides the door, in tears. Big tears are running down her cheeks. 'But how beautiful she is!', I say to myself."

"I then got closer to admire her better, Her eyes mostly attracted me... I looked, expecting that at any moment they would blink as the statue gave so much the impression to be alive."

"I then asked Joseph Francis if I could pick a tear that was on the verge of falling. With his consent I picked it up with my scapular and moistened my wedding rings at the same time asking this good Mother to bless our union and also my children."

86

"I then took out of my bag several religious articles which I put at her feet for her to bless. Joseph Francis made the sign of the cross with a tear on the forehead of my statue of the Holy Curé of Ars, and on another smaller statue belonging to my son Marc."

"What a ravishing beauty! I did not want to talk loudly for I had like the impression of being in a church. I felt an atmosphere which is beyond anything one can imagine."

"Her cheeks seemed so smooth that I asked permission to touch them… It is certainly not an ordinary statue. it is the most beautiful I had ever seen."

"Marc and I then talked for a few hours with Joseph Francis. The latter lives poorly, lacking much comfort, but he does not complain."

"Later before leaving we prayed with him. At departure time, my son asked to remain a few minutes alone with him. So I went out. About half an hour later he came out, and I found him happier than I had ever seen him for a long time. Joseph Francis had told him things that nobody, humanly speaking, could have known. By revealing to him these secrets, Joseph Francis opened Marc's eyes who, at the time, was walking a dangerous path."

"The next morning, on our way home, we say the rosary…"

January 31, 1985

Gaby Vienneau

13 - He Comes Back to Religious Practice

Following is the spontaneous testimonial made by young Marc Vienneau, age 20, son of Gaby and Eugene Vienneau, in a letter addressed to a priest, after a visit to Joseph Francis.

"Today something very special happened. For a certain time I was quite revolted following some events which had happened in the past year. I had discontinued going to church and any thought about religion disgusted me."

"A few days ago, I had to go on a trip to see a doctor. My mother and I took advantage of this to pay a visit to Joseph Francis, whose statue sheds tears. The idea did not please me at first."

"Upon entering we are welcomed by an odor of roses, and then we see the statue. She was crying."

"I had the chance to talk in private with Joseph Francis, and he told me things that nobody else knew. As he talked to me, he often looked at the statue as if the Virgin was telling him what to tell me."

"I had never felt so great a presence of the Blessed Virgin. I was not revolted anymore (against religion). My life was changed."

"Before this, I had not understood why the statue wept, but now I do. She weeps because her children are astray and have no one to show them the road to heaven."

"I also felt other emotions that I am at a loss to explain..."

January 31, 1985   *Marc Vienneau*

In her personal testimonial, the mother does add:

"... It is Marc who asked me to recite the rosary. It was his first since last September!"

14 - I Was Changed

"The first time I saw the statue weep, was on Friday, October 26, 1984, during an evening of prayer. The first thing I noticed, as I entered the house where the statue of Mary was, was a strong odor of rose which prevailed. I looked around, looking for flowers. And I asked: 'Where are the roses?'"

"I was answered that the fragrance was coming from the tears of the Blessed Virgin."

"I said laughing: 'What kind of joke is this?'"

"While saying this, I looked up at the statue. And there indeed were tears streaming down her face and falling on her hands."

"A funny thought crossed my mind. I did think this was arranged."

"As you see then, I did not believe on the spot. I really thought that it was just a bad joke, and I could not accept that such a joke be made about the Marian devotion. Since my conversion to Catholicism 24 years ago, Mary and the Rosary was a fortress in my spiritual life."

"After watching the tears flow for about half an hour, I decided to approach the statue to touch it and pray. 'Mary', I said, 'if all this is true, give me a sign that it is all real'. A little later I went back to her and prayed that my husband and my six boys be protected."

"That night, Mary did give me a sign."

"Before the end of the meeting, a man in the group said that someone needed prayers. I understood that the Blessed Virgn was telling me that someone was suffering. I was the one suffering as I feared at the time for my marriage..."

"Some friends in the group knelt and started to pray to my intentions. And I prayed alongside. Then I felt something happened inside me. My heart was changed. And the witness, Joseph Francis learned the sufferings I was going through. I felt a great peace inside of me."

"I noticed something else. Up till then, according to the expression that the statue had, Mary seemed to be looking at the floor, but at a given moment she seemed to stare right into my eyes."

"That night I did not sleep. Around 5 a.m. I thought I saw a woman with a baby at the foot of my bed. I tried to wake up my husband but without success. For four months I often thought about the baby I had lost before term 25 years ago."

"Was it the fruit of our union that heaven had asked us to offer then, and that the Blessed Virgin now carried in her heart?"

"I believe that Our Lady really weeps through the statue of Joseph Francis, and that through her, that night, I had received favors and consolation."

November 5, 1984   *Mrs. J.R.*

15 - I Cried with Our Lady

"On October 26, I went to a friend's place to recite the rosary with a group. It was with joy that I had accepted the invitation. I was told then that there was the possibility of having the presence of the statue of Our Lady that weeps."

"When I arrived, there were already many people around the statue and I said to myself: 'What a beautiful statue! She has the most beautiful countenance of the Virgin that I have ever seen.' As I was being introduced to some people, I was about four feet from the Virgin, and I felt myself enveloped by a cloud of rose fragrance. I looked around to see where the flowers were, but there were none. The scent disappeared for a few minutes, but I smelled roses again. It was definite and very pronounced. It was then that I asked aloud: 'Where are the flowers? I smell the fragrance of roses!'"

"Someone in the group simply said: 'It is the tears of Our Lady.' I got closer to the statue and noticed that indeed the Blessed Virgin was shedding tears. Her eyes were very beautiful, but sad, and her countenance expressed sorrow."

"It is not easy for me to express my feelings. I started to cry. I cried because I felt her sorrow. I cried because I thought I was privileged to be a witness to this miracle, knowing my unworthiness. I cried because of the loss of souls, the sceptics, the unbelievers."

"Following this event, a friend asked me if my life had changed because of that. Yes, I believe so…"

"I received more interior peace and also, although it seems contradictory, I feel an urgent need to bring others to Jesus through the Heart of Mary, the Heart of our so loving and perfect Mother."

"I received the grace to take more time each day for prayer and place my imperfect prayers in the Immaculate Heart of Mary. My personal intention have become Mary's intentions."

"Before witnessing this event, I had already consecrated myself to the Immaculate Heart of Mary. Nevertheless, that evening, I consecrated myself again in front of the statue, by touching her hand and looking at her eyes drowned with the tears of my Mother. My impression? I feel totally ablaze with love, oblation, and united by an unbreakable bond."

"My Mystical Rose! I smelled roses…"

March 1985   *Gail Stephen*

16 - Our Lady on the Conquest of Souls

"I had sent a package to a friend residing in Norway."

"Some time later, I received through Joseph Francis a message from the Blessed Virgin saying that my dispatch 'had saved the soul of my friend'. I learned that this friend, after having taken note of what I had sent her 'had cried all day long, and had felt repentance for all her life away from God'."

"Then a letter dated the day that has been indicated to me arrives and confirms the message."

" 'The photos that you have sent', she writes, 'are a treasure… I have finally been able to listen to the cassette Sunday when everything was quiet, and never have I appreciated anything like it.' "

"The photos she talked about were those of Our Lady in tears. And besides healing songs, the tape included two messages by the Virgin to her beloved Sons, the recitation of the rosary, and some readings."

"'I had a knot in the throat', she adds, 'and I listened so closely that I did not hear anything else.'"

"Thank you so much! I know that I shall listen to it again. I also shall read the books, and I am anxious to do so. Thank you also for the beautiful beads. Thank you for having taken the time to do all this for me, Gail, it was what I needed the most.'"

"It is Our Lady who used me to do that. All during the taping, I asked Our Lady to touch her heart. It was certainly what she did as one can see by the content of my friend's letter. This person is the mother of one of my godsons."

"Joseph Francis told me that her husband would also benefit from the graces that she had received."

April 1985   *Gail Stephen*

IV

OUR ANSWER

How shall we answer the tears of the Virgin?

How to answer the tears of such a good Mother?

But first: how not to be moved by the tears of the Mother of God?

Tears of compassion, there, at the foot of the cross, where Her crucified Son is dying for the redemption of mankind.

Tears of supplication for so many souls who refuse redemption.

Tears of reparation for this unending flow of sins and crimes of all kinds that a sinful humanity does not cease to breed.

Tears of comfort for so much human suffering: physical suffering of those who groan in their bodies; moral suffering for so much hate and egoism which reach her children in their innerself; incomprehensible suffering for the immense crowd of the infidels who ignore everything of salvation, of the road which leads to it and the redeeming value of accepted and offered suffering.

All these tears shed in the world, the Immaculate Heart of Mary *participates* in them, *shares* them, *blesses* them, *sanctifies* them, *assumes* them by *offering* them to the Father, so that they may be offerings of *reparation* and *supplication.*

These two aspects of the suffering of Mary, she recalls them herself in one of the messages to Don Stefano Gobbi, of Milan:

The Compassion

She first recalls how she participates in the suffering of Her crucified Son:

"And now my sorrow bursts forth as a flooding river bursts through all its embankments. My tears bathe his face, my laments cradle his body and with my hands I close the deep wounds, while my Immaculate Heart becomes his first sepulchre." (1)

The Co-Redemption

If the Mother of God participates so closely to the mystery of Redemption, she also contributes closely to the suffering of those who are called to cooperate to the Redemption. Is she not the Co-Redemptrix?

In the same message, she tells us that her place today is still here, near all her sons, in order to share our suffering and offer them to the Father:

"Till the end of the world, I will always be close to you, sons begotten of the death of my only Son."

"Above all, I am with you during these moments of darkness and suffering, when you are being called to live out what Jesus endured during his redemptive passion."

"I am always near you to help you to suffer, to die and to rise again, that the plan of the Father be fulfilled and that, with Jesus, you too may rejoice in the glory of his Kingdom of life." (2)

Unfortunately man does not answer this love, or so little! The Virgin complains about it, she expresses her anxiety:

"Are you not aware of how I am summoning you from all sides, gathering you together and pleading with you? I am imploring you with signs which are becoming greater and more numerous: my tears, my apparitions, my messages." (3)

In 1976, Theresa Musco, a stigmatic victim-soul trained at Our Lady's school of the cross, died at the age of 33, in Italy. Concerning the multiple divine manifestations which marked her short life, Don Franco Amico, pastor of one of the parishes where she has lived, and member of the study committee of *Theresa Musco,* writes the following:

"But then, we have not yet undestood anything of the apparitions of La Salette, Lourdes, Fatima, and of the tears of Syracuse.Do we not see that there is an increase of impressive manifestations? We pretend as if it is all about nothing, and we are in search of alibis..."

"The Madonna herself in her messages to Theresa does nothing else but beseech her children maternally, especially the privileged ones, for a sincere return to God, and to live in his grace and his love." (4)

The numerous messages given by Our Lady to Theresa Musco are tied to those which the Virgin in tears give in Canada. In a thick volume consecrated to this CRUCIFIED WITH THE CRUCIFIED (the title of the book), Father Gabriel Roschini, a famous mariologist, relates the following words that the Blessed Virgin told Theresa, on January 3, 1952:

"I want to tell you that the world is terribly bad... I appeared in Lourdes and in La Salette, but very few are the obstinate hearts who converted themselves... I appeared in Portugal, bringing messages, and nobody has listened to me..." (5)

The Real Marian Devotion...

We are still questioning about the real Marian devotion as if it entailed defining the love of Our Lady, and what should be our answer, the while calling us to conversion, she speaks, moans, and sheds abundant tears in front of human indifference and ingratitude.

This is not time to *define* but to *answer* her heart rending calls through prayer, conversion of the heart, reparation and apostolate.

The real Marian devotion, today, in this Marian epoch which must bring the triumph of the Immaculate Heart of Mary, consists in listening to what is told us by the Mother descended from Heaven in order to be close to us, and make her anguished calls of her Sorrowful and Immaculate Heart heard more closely by a humanity with a stiff neck.

Let us stop quibbling around a too theoretical Marian devotion, *while the Mother is speaking,* the One Sent by the Father and the Son, to transmit to us a message of salvation. Let us *listen rather.* Let our heart be penetrated by these multiform calls of our Mother, and let us give the chance to this hardened or benumbed heart to be moved and transformed, as many faithfuls have already done.

... Leads to the Heart of Jesus

If we stop quibbling and listen to what She wants to say, we shall rapidly understand where the call of Mary leads: the Sorrowful and Immaculate Heart *calls us to plunge ourselves in the Sacred Heart of Jesus,* termination of Christian life and springboard to Paradise.

Here is an example of the goal and meaning of a true Marian devotion, drawn from the messages of the Virgin to her beloved sons:

"My dearly beloved son, turn with serenity to the Heart of Jesus."

"If you knew how much He loves you, how He looks on you with predilection! Do you know why? Because you continue to be so small, so poor, so full of defects..."

"Cast everything into the burning furnace of his Heart and everything will be burned up in his merciful Love: your sins, your weaknesses, your defects."

"In the end, nothing of yourself will remain: the good you do will be our work alone. You will offer us that gift which is, to us, the most precious and which we always want from you: your love."

"You can love us this way too: in littleness, in poverty, in your truly great misery."

"Do not become discouraged when you find that you promise Me something and then do not keep to it..."

"You have however offered Me your sorrow and regret for your error and my motherly Heart leaps for joy because of this."

"Nevertheless you should also strive to observe whatever I ask of you and to keep to what you promise Me."

"Silence with everyone, prayer, suffering and the greatest confidence in Me."

"These intimate sufferings, these secret humiliations of yours, make you similar to my Crucified Son. Let yourself be made more and more like Him by your heavenly Mother, who wants to adjust you well upon the cross, that cross which my Son Jesus has prepared for you..." (6)

A WORD FROM THE AUTHOR

I could be asked: "Have you, yourself, seen the Virgin weep? Have you smelled the fragrance?"

Concretely, my answer is, "No!". No more than I have seen the tomb of Christ ressurected, or the Lord in His Glory. No more than I have seem Him ascend to Heaven on Ascension day. No more than I have seen the tongues of fire settle down on the foreheads of the Apostles, and at the same time on that of the Mother of the Church, on Pentecostal day.

I have not seen any of that. But I believe because it is the belief of the Church, and the belief of the Church rests on FACTS and on the CREDIBILITY of the witnesses who have certified them.

And on the fruits which have followed the testimony or accompanied it.

Saint Peter would tell the people: "This Jesus hath God raised again, whereof all we are witnesses." (Acts 2, 32) What was the value of Peter's testimony? The *veracity* of the fact, the *sincerity* and the *loyalty* of the witness, and the *fruits* that were produced.

Answering the inspiration of the Holy Ghost and the testimony of these men, bearer of a word and a blessing, the crowds in the thousands have accepted baptism.

And the Church was born. And she has produced fruits of sanctity.

*** *** ***

We all know with what solicitude She surrounds this herd that the Father has given to the Son. And what is the considerable share the Mother takes today in looking after the interests of the Son.

Manifestations of all kinds which have been increasing without cease for a century and a half. Apparitions, messages, so many signs of her love and kindness. And always the souls of good-will, priests, religious and laymen, witnesses of her favors and beneficiaries of her gifts, repeat the word of Saint Peter: "All we are witnesses."

Shall I dare say, "Yes, I have seen!"? For I have seen more; I have sensed more; I have tasted more than those who have seen, sensed, tasted physically the tears...

The Most Holy Virgin has multiple ways of speaking. I have shown it further up. And the interior spiritual discourses are no less eloquent, no less effective, than the visible signs. God keep me from lessening in any way whatsoever the *visible signs* that this book has been consecrated to publish and have honored.

So what favor, what blessing for the one who, feeling unworthy of it all, has seen himself entrusted with such a deposit! To lend his trembling pen to the Queen of Heaven and earth, for the publication of her message and the transmission of the testimonial of her tears: what a grace and a blessing!

What a blessing to feel underneath each fact, underneath each word which was entrusted me, underneath the words which were inspired to me, a *divine presence,* a *maternal warmth* covering and directing!

Yes, *I have felt* the Immaculate Heart of Our Mother beat: first in Her Work, and how not to believe what one feels deep oneself? I felt it beat in the hearts of those who have pooled their efforts, their resources, thus permitting the publication of this work in two languages.

Yes, *I have seen* the tears of the Madonna shine in the eyes of those who have testified: tears of compassion, tears of affection, tears of the joy of feeling so close to us The One who is at the same time so close to God and so powerful on His Heart!

Yes, *I have sensed* the delicate fragrance of the celestial Mother manifest itself under the delicate gestures of collaboration, without which I was powerless. The fragrance of the Virgin, is that of her virtues. And this fragrance is manifest or manifests itself with those who let themselves be touched, who accept to put themselves at her service and under her guidance.

Yes, *I have seen* the Virgin smile close to me through those who serve her. *I have tasted* the gentleness of her Love in the detachment and abandonment of these generous souls, the small circle of the consecrated ones to the Immaculate Heart whose detachment and generosity enabled me to proceed to the end.

Yes, *I have seen* the Madonna animate her countenance on the dozens of photographs that are shown in this book. *Suffering countenance* of the Co-Redemptrix; *serene countenance* of an encouraging Mother; *severe countenance* of the Victorious One, Who makes the Wicked One flee, always on the lookout to trip us.

Her countenance of compassion, consolation, encouragement and protection, that has already conquered the small number, now turns towards the great number of her children.

It is up to you, who will let yourselves be touched, who will want to welcome in your hearts the graces that the Virgin offers in this LAST CALL, to you then, to transmit it around you, for the Glory of God, the triumph of the Immaculate Heart of Mary, and the salvation of the greater number!

June 19, 1985
    Feast of the
       Immaculate Heart of Mary   Jean-Yves Simard

TO COME

It will be understood that with the first book the subject matter is not exhaustive, far from it. Many other signs (facts) had to be put aside giving all the space to the animated statue of Our Lady of Fatima.

From the start it had been envisioned to treat separately and in detail the other manifestations of the Mother of God, those of Her Son Jesus and those of other celestial messengers whose essential aim is to awaken the faith and establish in the hearts docility and submission to God.

A second book is therefore in preparation, and this to conform ourselves to the urgent requests of Our Lord and Our Lady.

Those who have been moved by the reading of this "Last Call" are invited to make it known, thus multiplying the number of beneficiaries of the blessings largely offered to the souls of good will.

The volume which will follow will thus be a sequel to the present work. With the narrative of facts, will be offered to inward contemplation and pious consideration:

1) Different colored photos of
   - a weeping statue of the Sacred Heart,
   - a crucifix shedding blood,
   - a weeping image of Christ crucified,
   - a weeping bust of Christ crowned with thorns,
   - a weeping image of the Sacred Heart,
   - a weeping Infant Jesus lying in the manger;

2) Different photos of the Madonna in tears, through
   - another statue of Our Lady of Fatima, in Fatima,
   - a statue of Our Lady with the Child, in Sienna,
   - an image of the Virgin in White with the Child,
   - an image of Our Lady of Perpetual Help.

3) Photos of a magnificent weeping statue of St. Joseph with the Christ Child also in tears,

4) Photos of other manifestations such as
   - a weeping image of the Holy Father,
   - a weeping statue of St. Cecilia,
   - a weeping image of St. Francis of Assisi,
   - a weeping image of Padre Pio.

It is thus important for the glory of God and the salvation of souls to give a sequel to the reading of this first volume and remain in close relationship with Our Lord and His Blessed Mother. The pious knowledge of these facts and the prayers of reparation which ensue are sources of graces for the reader, his family and near relations, as well as to those to whom he will wish to transmit the message.

APPENDIX I
THE MOST HOLY HEARTS OF JESUS AND MARY

Following the requests made to Saint Margaret-Mary by Jesus Himself, in the XVIIth century, the *devotion to the Sacred Heart* was established in the Church. In 1917 in Fatima, the Blessed Virgin asked Lucy to work towards establishing the *devotion to Her Immaculate Heart.*

How could the Sacred Heart of Jesus and the Sorrowful and Immaculate Heart of Mary not be united? How could these two devotions not be closely associated?

It is the authorized and official teaching of the Catholic Church that, for example, we find under the pen of this great doctor that was His Holiness Pope Pius XII:

"In order that in the Christian family and in all of mankind more abundant fruits derive from the cult of the most sacred Heart of Jesus, the faithful must see to associate it closely to the cult towards the Immaculate Heart of Mary. By divine will the blessed Virgin Mary was undissolvably united to Christ in the work of human Redemption,so that our salvation come from the love and sufferings of Jesus Christ undissolvably united to the love and sorrows of his mother. This is why it is perfectly suitable that the Christian people, who have received divine life of Christ through Mary, after having given the cult due to the most sacred Heart of Jesus, also give to the most loving Heart of his celestial Mother similar homage of piety, love, gratitute and reparation."

(Haurietis aquas, May 15, 1956)

Having thus theologically defined the close relationship between the two devotions, Pius XII points out in the same document how this practice can be beneficial to all:

"To the sinful souls, to those suffering from their faults, to those wanting to expiate the sins of others, the devotion to the Sorrowful and Immaculate Heart, the Heart of their Mother, seems as a haven both of ideal and forgiveness."

(Ibid)

Hence it is the Will of the Lord Himself that we venerate, pray and love both the Heart of his Mother and His.

"The world must be consecrated to the Sorrowful and Immaculate Heart as it is to Mine. Do not fear whatever suffering or obstacle that you may meet: only think of accomplishing my will."

(Words of Our Lord to Berthe Petit, Summer of 1910)

"The two Hearts appeared more than once to Berthe Petit not close together in a reciprocal embrace of love but copenetrating each other as if soldered together in and by one ardent flame of charity."

(Father Colin, c.s.s.r., Berthe Petit Apôtre du Coeur Douloureux et Immaculé de Marie, Nouvelles Éditions Latines, Paris, 1967, p. 38-39)

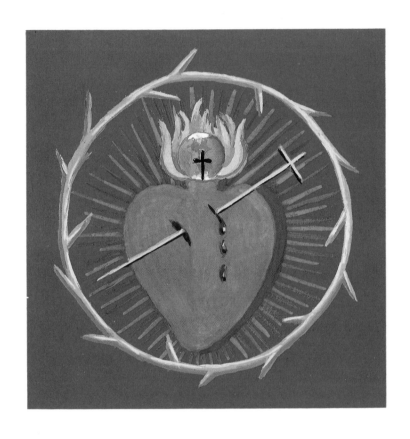

"Behold the Heart of your Mother."
"My heart is Her Heart; we cannot separate them, for they are One,
as My Father and I are One."

*"In spirit My Heart and the Immaculate Heart of Mary are One, where
any heart has a refuge of safety.
So the spirit of the human heart is protected in both Our Hearts. We Three
are One."*
                                          (Message from Our Lord)

APPENDIX II

OUR LADY SPEAKS TO HER BELOVED PRIESTS

Zompitta (Udine)
January 24, 1984

My Signs

"Beloved sons, I welcome this Rosary you are reciting together with such great love and fervor.

As a mother I wish to speak to you, I who am here with you, represented by the statue you have here. Every statue of mine is a sign of my presence, and reminds you of your heavenly Mother. Therefore each of them should be honored and put in a place of greater veneration.

Just as you look with love at a photograph of a cherished person because it transmits to you a reminder and a likeness, so too you should look with love at every image of your heavenly Mother, because it transmits to you a reminder of Her, or rather it becomes a particular sign of her presence among you.

How deeply saddened I am by the circumstance, today so frequent, of being ousted from the churches. Sometimes I am placed outside, in a corridor, like some trinket; sometimes I am put in the back of the church, so that none of my children can see or venerate Me.

A sign also of how much I like the fitting veneration given to my images is what I am effecting through this little statue. It is a triple sign I give you: that of my eyes, which suddenly come alive; that of the color of my countenance, which changes its hue; and that of my Heart, which exudes a fragrance, now a delicate one, now one of greater strength.

By the sign I give you in the eyes, I want to show you that your heavenly Mother, never so much as in these times, is watching you with merciful eyes. She is never far from you; she takes cognizance of you in all the difficulties in which you find yourselves, in the difficult moments you are living, with all the sufferings besetting you, with the great cross you must carry.

And with these eyes I look at all, at those far away, at the atheists, at the drug addicts, at my poor sinful children, to know them just as they are, to guide them along the path of goodness, of a return to God, of conversion, prayer, fasting and penance.

102

In a particular way I look at you, my beloved, objects of my maternal complacency. Especially you, beloved of my sacerdotal Movement, who form for Me an object of great gratification.

I look at you and I illumine you with my own beauty. In you I reflect the candor of Heaven that is mine. You should be lilies in your purity, roses in your fragrance, cyclamens in your littleness. In this way you compose this beautiful crown of love that makes the thorny crown of my sorrow break into blossom.

By the sign I give you in the color of my visage, I want to show you that I am a Mother for all, and today I share in all your needs, and I rejoice in all your joys. But I also suffer in all your numerous sufferings.

When a mother is happy and jumps for joy, you see the color of her face become rosy; when she is worried about the fate of her children, you see her face turn completely pale. If this happens to an earthly mother, it also happens to Me, and the sign I give you, so human and maternal, is to tell you that as a Mother I truly share in all the moments of your mortal life.

When you suffer, I suffer. When you rejoice, I rejoice. When you are good, I jump for joy. When you love Me, my face is all aflame because of the joy you give Me.

By the sign I give you with the fragrance I exude, sometimes of lesser, sometimes of greater strength, I wish to show you that I am always among you, but especially when you are more in need of Me.

If you do not recognize the perfume, or you notice it in a very faint way, it is not because I do not love you, or because you are wicked. A mother loves even with merciful predilection those who have the greater need for her!

Understand then why my maternal compassion goes out to sinners, all, but especially those who are furthest away, those most in need of Divine Mercy. Appearing at Fatima, I taught you to pray to Jesus in this way. 'Bring all souls to Heaven, especially those most in need of thy mercy'.

I love all, beginning with the furthest away, those of my children who are sinners, for whom I am a secure and maternal refuge.

Look at my merciful eyes which shed tears of sorrow and compassion. In so many parts of the world I give this sign, causing copious tears to stream my eyes, even tears of blood.

To give a sign of my maternal presence, and to accord to your lives a secure support, and amid the tribulations you are living, to call you to joy and to trust, in so many parts of the world I am still giving my maternal messages. They announce to you the certitude that I am following you and am with you. I live with you, I prepare everything for you, I lead you by the hand along the difficult road of this time of purification.

A fragrant sign of my maternal presence is to be found in the apparitions I am still making in many regions of the world. Yes, in these times I am appearing in Europe, in Asia, in Africa, in America, and in distant Oceania. The whole world is wrapped in my maternal mantle.

In the struggle, now conclusive, between Me and my Adversary, my extraordinary presence tells you that my victory has already begun. My beloved sons, how much I love you!

From you, to whom I have given so much, this I ask; that you increase your love for Me! (...)"

Our Lady Speaks to Her Beloved Priests,
The Marian Movement of Priests, Milan,
Supplement to the 7th English Edition, p. 413,
Message of January 24, 1984.

Translator's Note

The translation was completed surprisingly on the Feast of the Most Precious Blood, July 1, 1985.

This date of completion was not foreseen, and like the date of completion of writing by the author it coincides with one of the major feasts of the Church regarding the Sacred Heart and the Immaculate Heart of Mary, for the feast of the Most Precious Blood of Jesus is also a feast of Our Celestial Mother from whose Heart was drawn the Most Precious Blood of Jesus.

Br. Joseph Matthew

NOTES

Chapter I

THE CAUSE OF MY TEARS

1. Our Lady Speaks to Her Beloved Priests. The Marian Movement of Priests, Milan. Supplement to the 7th English Edition, p. 413, Message of January 24, 1984. See appendix 2.
2. Ibid.
3. Idem, 7th English Edition, p. 103, Message of October 30, 1975.

Part II

Chapter 5

A) AN ANIMATED STATUE

1. Chanoine C. Barthas / P.G. Da Fonseca, Fatima Merveille Inouïe, Fatima-Editions, Toulouse, 1943, p. 40.
2. L'Apparition de la Très Sainte Vierge sur la Montagne de la Salette, le 19 septembre 1846. Extrait de l'Édition original de Lecce, aux Éditions St-Raphaël, Sherbrooke, Qué. pp. 29-30.
3. Shimura Tatsuya, La Vierge Marie pleure au Japon (Akita), Ed. du Parvis, 1985, pp. 13-14.
4. See appendix 2.

B) SHE CRIES WITH US AND OVER US

1. See appendix 2.
2. Shimura Tatsuya, Akita, op. cit. p. 13. (See no. 3 above in Part II)
3. Message of La Salette, p. 31, (See no. 2 above in Part II)

C) THE LANGUAGE OF THE VIRGINAL FRAGRANCE

1. Lumière pour les âmes consacrées. Message de Padre Pio. Pro Manuscripto privatim, Casa di Padre Dio, St-Rémi, Qué., pp. 18-19.
2. Marie André, La magnifique histoire de Notre-Dame du Puy, Centre marial canadien, Nicolet, Qué., p. 3.

3. F. Léonard, F.S.C., Quand Marie apparaît, L'Étoile de la jeunesse, Rodez, 1953, p. 61. Also: Pierre Molaine, L'Itinéraire de la Vierge Marie, Correa, Paris, 1953, pp. 105, 110.
4. Barthas/Fonseca, Fatima, Merveille inouïe, pp. 73-74. (See no. 1 above, Part 1 section (a))
5. Père G. Hermes, Les larmes de Marie, Rose mystique, Eu. du Parvis, 1985, p. 5.

D) MYSTERIOUS PHOTOS

1. Mélanie, Message of La Salette, op. cit. pp. 32-33. (See no. 2 above in Part II)
2. Chanoine Barthas... op. cit. p. 39, on Fatima (See no. 1 above, Part II)
3. Idem, p. 53.
4. (See no. 1, p. 28)
5. (See no. 2, p. 40)

E) SHE PASSES DOING GOOD

1. See *Favors Obtained* at the beginning of this volume.

Part III

ONE MONTH WITH THE PILGRIM VIRGIN

1. See appendix 2. Message of January 24, 1984.
2. Idem.

Part IV

OUR ANSWER

1. Message of April 13, 1979, p. 244. (See no. 3, Part I)
2. Ibid.
3. Message of January 21, 1978, p. 197. (See no. 3. Part I)
4. R.P. Mondrone, Centre d'Études Apostoliques Mariales: Theresa Musco et les larmes de sang. p. 6.
5. Idem, p. 9.
6. Message of January 6, 1978, p. 196. (See no. 3, Part I)

CONTENTS

Printed and Bound
For the Feast of
Our Lady of Sorrows
September 15, 1985
By
Les Impressions J.L. Inc.
Beauport